CRE

CRETE

AMAZING
EXPERIENCES

DISCOVERY
TOURS

PULL-OUT
MAP

Travel with
**Insider
Tips**

MARCO POLO TOP HIGHLIGHTS

CHANIÁ OLD TOWN ⭐1
This is Crete in a nutshell: history and joie de vivre, art and good Mediterranean cuisine in between high mountain ranges and the Aegean Sea.
📷 *Tip: At dusk, step onto one of the boats at the Mosque of the Janissaries and take your pictures from the water!*

➤ p. 44, Chaniá

ELAFONÍSI BEACH ⭐2
The white sand and turquoise sea are reminiscent of the South Pacific, and the shallow water makes it a perfect beach for children.

➤ p. 54, Chaniá

VENETIAN HARBOUR ⭐3
At Crete's most beautiful harbour front, in Réthimno's old town, María's Knossós taverna serves delicious freshly caught fish.
📷 *Tip: The harbour is at its most picturesque when the lights come on in the evening and the crumbling render becomes almost unnoticeable.*

➤ p. 63, Réthimno

ARKÁDI MONASTERY ⭐4
Freedom or death? In this Venetian monastery, the besieged Cretans gave the Ottomans a gruesome answer to the question.
📷 *Tip: Drive 500m in the direction of Klissídi for the best views of the monastery.*

➤ p. 69, Réthimno

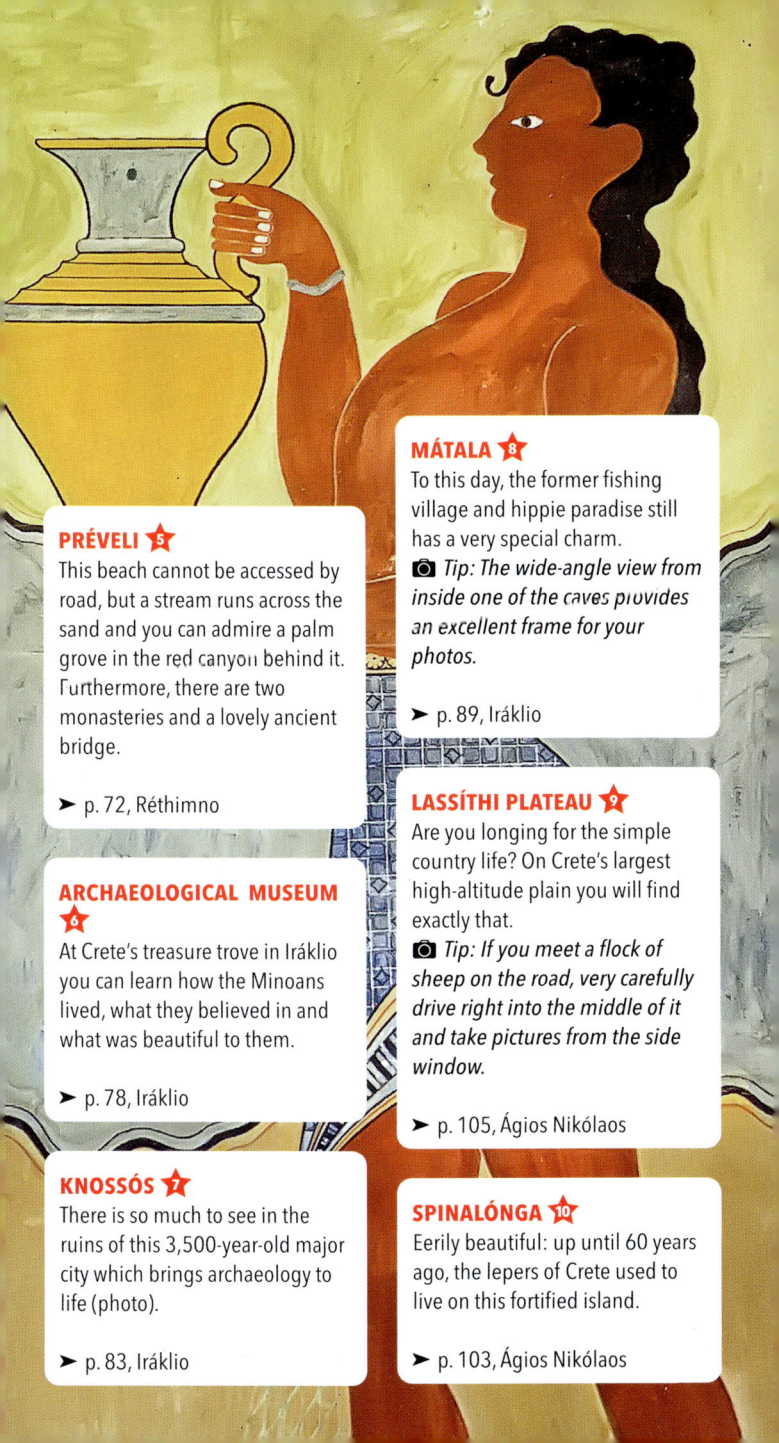

PRÉVELI ⭐5

This beach cannot be accessed by road, but a stream runs across the sand and you can admire a palm grove in the red canyon behind it. Furthermore, there are two monasteries and a lovely ancient bridge.

➤ p. 72, Réthimno

ARCHAEOLOGICAL MUSEUM ⭐6

At Crete's treasure trove in Iráklio you can learn how the Minoans lived, what they believed in and what was beautiful to them.

➤ p. 78, Iráklio

KNOSSÓS ⭐7

There is so much to see in the ruins of this 3,500-year-old major city which brings archaeology to life (photo).

➤ p. 83, Iráklio

MÁTALA ⭐8

To this day, the former fishing village and hippie paradise still has a very special charm.
📷 *Tip: The wide-angle view from inside one of the caves provides an excellent frame for your photos.*

➤ p. 89, Iráklio

LASSÍTHI PLATEAU ⭐9

Are you longing for the simple country life? On Crete's largest high-altitude plain you will find exactly that.
📷 *Tip: If you meet a flock of sheep on the road, very carefully drive right into the middle of it and take pictures from the side window.*

➤ p. 105, Ágios Nikólaos

SPINALÓNGA ⭐10

Eerily beautiful: up until 60 years ago, the lepers of Crete used to live on this fortified island.

➤ p. 103, Ágios Nikólaos

CONTENTS

CONTENTS

⊙	Plan your visit	🍴	Eating/drinking	🐾	Family activities
€–€€€	Price categories	👜	Shopping	🚩	Classic experiences
(*)	Premium-rate phone number	🍸	Going out	✦	Sustainable activities
		🌴	Top beaches	✓	Marco Polo bucket list
		🐗	Budget activities		

(📖 A2) Refers to the removable pull-out map
(0) Located off the map

Réthimno

BEST OF CRETE

It's hard to imagine a more idyllic scene than the lagoon at Bálos Beach

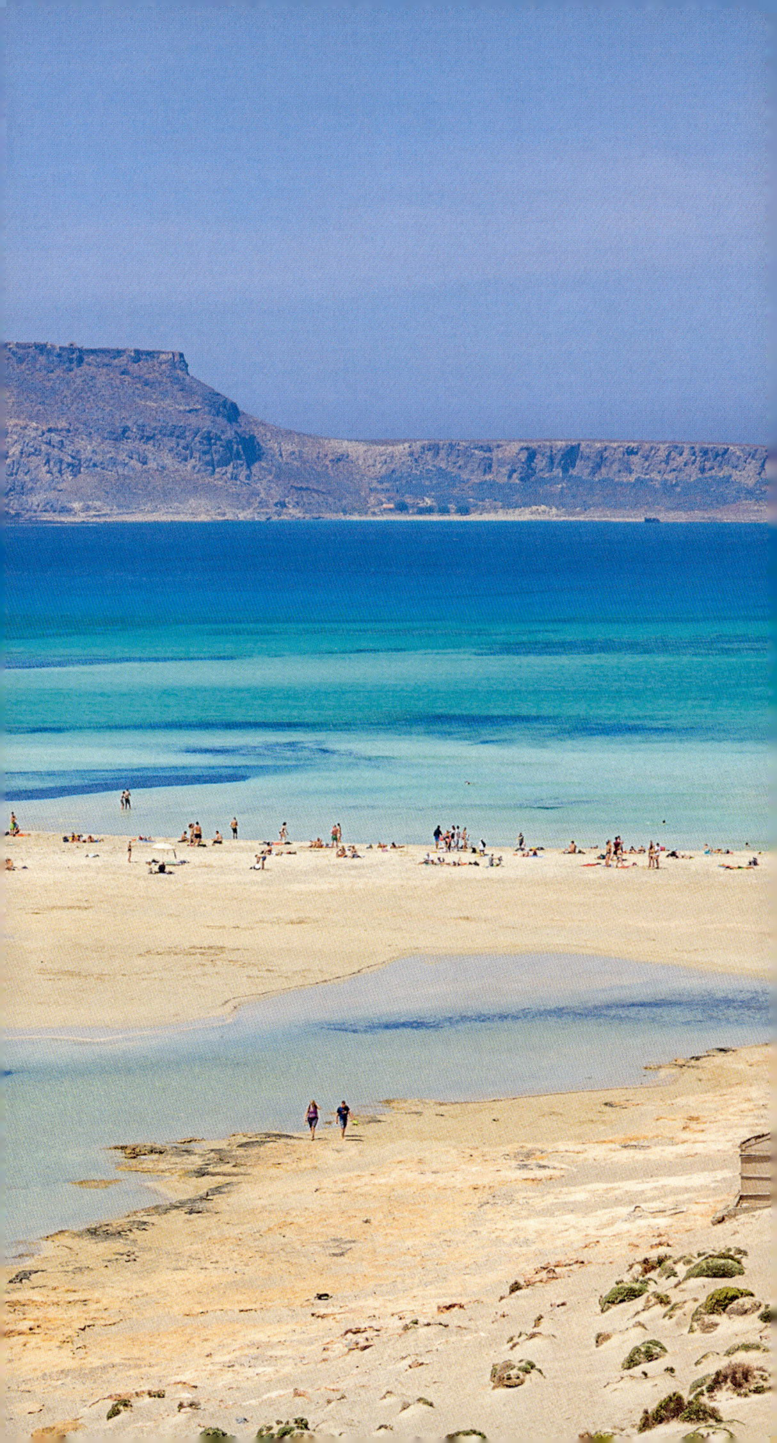

BEST

GREEN & FAIR

EAT LOCAL PRODUCE

An all-inclusive package may be convenient, but don't miss the chance to visit a local taverna that serves the island's produce. In doing so, you'll be supporting many family businesses. You could try the juice produced from the fruit trees that grow in the *Botanical Park of Crete*, or the regional vegetables grown on the *Lassíthi Plateau*.

➤ p. 52, Chaniá, p. 105 Ágios Nikólaos

DIRECT FROM THE ARTIST

By buying traditional crafts you're not just extending your holiday memories; you're also supporting Cretan artists and artisans. In *Margarítes* there is a cluster of over 20 pottery studios, selling unique items at a decent price.

➤ p. 70, Réthimno

TASTE CRETAN WINES

There are many Cretan wines that could hold their own against most better-known international labels. Sample them in the island's tavernas or, best of all, alongside the vintner at a local vineyard; there are a few in and around *Archánes*.

➤ p. 84, Iráklio

FARMERS' MARKETS

If you're self-catering or just preparing a picnic lunch, be sure to visit the *weekly markets* in Crete's towns, where the island's fruit and veg are sold at a good price. The Saturday market in *Míres* is one of the best.

➤ p. 92, Iráklio

TAKE THE BUS

Crete's most popular holiday destinations – *Plataniás* and *Agía Marína* to the west; *Chersónisos* and *Mália* to the east – are well-connected by bus to Chaniá and Iráklio respectively. So there's no need to hire a car for a trip into town or worry about finding a parking space.

➤ p. 149, Good to know

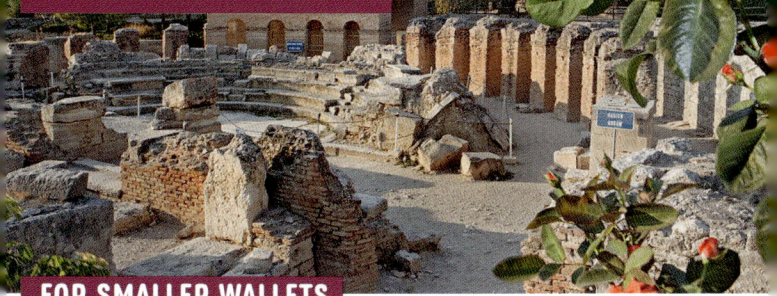

BEST 🐷
ON A BUDGET

FOR SMALLER WALLETS

ADMISSION FREE
Admission to all the excavation sites and archaeological museums on Crete is free on 6 March, 18 April, 18 May as well as the last weekend in September and 28 October each year. It's also free on the first Sunday of each month between November and March.

WHERE THE OLIVE OIL FLOWS
The young proprietor of the *Paráskákis olive oil factory* will show you the secrets of harvesting olive oil, and you can also go on a free guided tour of the ultra-modern facility in Melidóni.
➤ p. 70, Réthimno

FREE ADMISSION TO THE POOL
Admission prices into waterparks are usually extremely expensive but you can enter the *Star Beach Water Park* in Liménas Chersónisou for free. You only pay to ride the slides.
➤ p. 86, Iráklio

FREE CONCERTS
Admission to all the concerts held at the *Mátala Beach Festival* is free. The streets become canvases for artworks and the beach pulsates with music.
➤ p. 90, Iráklio

RUINS IN AN OLIVE GROVE
After seeing the Odéon and Títus Basilica of Górtis, opt to continue on a lovely walk through the ruins of the Roman city in age-old olive groves, which, unlike the excavations on the opposite side of the road – are free of charge (photo).
➤ p. 93, Iráklio

BY BUS INSTEAD OF CAR
There is an excellent public bus network on Crete which connects almost all villages on the island. Prices are low: from as little as 1.80 euros you can get to the nearest beach by bus.
➤ p. 149, Good to know

BEST

WITH CHILDREN

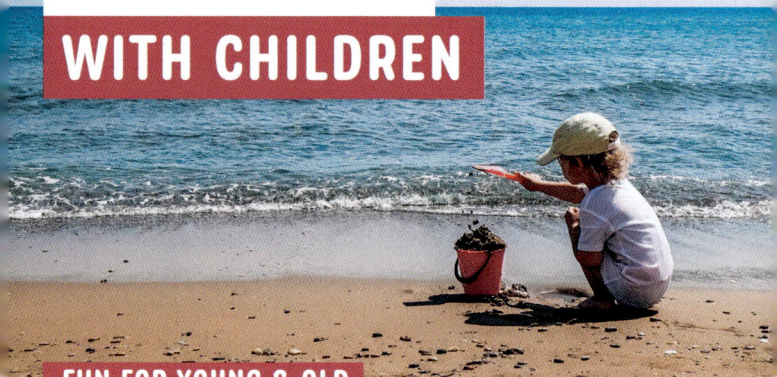

TAKE A MINI TRAIN

Choo-choo – here comes the train! And although it's not a full-sized train that rolls along proper tracks, it does have a *motorised engine* with three open carriages and it rides along many of the streets on rubber tyres. Check out the train timetable in Georgioúpoli.

➤ p. 51, Chaniá

WALK WITH DONKEYS

Arno de Vrij is the *donkey whisperer* of Crete. Listen to his entertaining anecdotes about these animals as you accompany (rather than ride) the donkeys on a nature ramble in Georgioúpoli.

➤ p. 51, Chaniá

SAILING WITH PIRATES

Have Lego pirates taken over your bedroom at home? Then it's high time you treat your children to a trip on the *Captain Hook* pirate ship. It is moored in Réthimno harbour and is waiting for a crew of little sailors.

➤ p. 66, Réthimno

UNDERSEA INHABITANTS

The *Cretaquarium* in Goúrnes is *the* most state-of-the-art aquarium in Greece. More than 2,000 sea creatures are housed here, including octopuses, lobsters, seahorses and sharks. It's a hit with kids.

➤ p. 85, Iráklio

DON'T GET LOST!

Follow the trail of the Minotaur through the maze at the *Labyrinth Park* near Chersónisos. If you find the exit, you gain access to a game of minigolf! Unfortunately, all other activities, such as The Underworld and the Laser Maze–Trojan Horse, cost extra, but they are a lot of fun.

➤ p. 86, Iráklio

BEST ⚑
CLASSIC EXPERIENCES

ONLY ON CRETE

THE SOUND OF LYRES IN CHANIÁ

The *lýra* and *laoúto* are Crete's traditional musical instruments. Every night you can hear them being played in *Adéspoto* in Chaniá's old town, for locals and foreign guests. The lyrics are mostly about love and the fight for freedom.
➤ p. 49, Chaniá

RAKÍ & MEZÉDES

When *mezédes* (photo) are served, your table will be laden with a variety of small dishes. As an accompaniment, Cretans love to drink *rakí* from small decanters. The ideal venue for this is a *rakádika*; there are a number of them squeezed into the *Odós Vernárdou* in Réthimno.
➤ p. 63, Réthimno

NIGHTLIFE IN IRÁKLIO

In the street cafés surrounding the *Odós Milátou,* mostly young Cretans sit on funky lounge furniture, meet their friends and listen to music. Iced coffee is the most popular drink.
➤ p. 83, Iráklio

SURROUNDED BY MOUNTAINS

Uninhabited plateaux are a geographical feature of the island. During the summer countless sheep and goats graze here, and during the winter they are covered in snow. The *Nída Plateau,* just under the summit of Mount Psilorítis, is easy to reach and beautiful for walking.
➤ p. 88, Iráklio

BACK TO THE HIPPIES

Mátala became famous in the 1960s, when hippies came from all over the world to live here. Every year in late June/early July, the spirit of Woodstock is rekindled during the *Mátala Beach Festival.* The stage is set up on the beach, with a campsite right behind it. The music unites all generations.
➤ p. 90, Iráklio

GET TO KNOW CRETE

Octopus is gutted and cleaned in Chaniá harbour

DISCOVER CRETE

Inland Crete, with its villages and monasteries, is as varied as the island's coastline

Approaching Crete from the air, it becomes obvious that this island is essentiallly a vast, high mountain range in the middle of the sea. Its beaches are more of a sideshow, and only a few paces inland you begin to discover one of the most unspoilt and varied islands in Europe.

UNSPOILT VILLAGES

Don't miss the southern part of the island, where the old fort of Frangokastéllo stands guard over a wide sandy beach. From here, a narrow road winds up the steep slope like the thread of a corkscrew. A few houses are scattered down below, in the glowing sun on the coastal plain. Beyond, the sea doesn't reach land again until Libya. There is a touch of Africa in the air – and occasionally dust from the Sahara. A rustic *kafenío* dozes in the sun at the entrance to the first mountain village you come to. The landlord, Bábis, has decorated the airy terrace with goat

1900–1450 BCE Minoan era. Palaces of Knossós, Festós, Mália	**1450–480 BCE** Greek tribes settle on Crete. About 100 independent city states are founded	**480 BCE–CE 395** Classical, Hellenistic and Roman eras	**395–1204** Byzantine era. Constantinople rules Crete	**1204–1669** Venetian era	**1669–1898** Ottoman era	**1898–1913** Crete is autonomous

skulls. His Danish partner, Janina, brews mountain tea and a lavender stalk floats on top of the lemonade. The herbs, jams and other regional products on offer make great souvenirs. The home-made wine tastes of Cretan soil. Here in Kallikrátis it is not very difficult to forget about the rest of the world.

Continue to another mountain village: Anógia. It is still early in the year. In the modest coffee shop on the town square wood is crackling in the fireplace. Chairs with woven seats line three of the walls. Against the fourth wall, behind the counter, the host brews rich coffee in brass and copper pots, pours it into small espresso cups and serves it to the guests with a glass of water. Just above the counter is a huge flat-screen television broadcasting an important football match. Everyone is watching and commentating. Then the half-time whistle. A guest turns off the television. Two young men, both in OFI Iráklio shirts, each grab a *lýra*, an age-old Cretan instrument, and begin playing and singing masterfully. The essence of Crete fills the room. After 15 minutes, the television is turned on again and the music stops. A fast-food chain advertises hamburgers, and then the soccer game continues.

MODERN TIMES

Time hasn't stood still on Crete. Gigantic wind turbines rotate on mountain ridges, and on the motorways and dual carriageways of the north coast, the Cretans rush from town to town. In Iráklio an EU institute takes care of data security for the whole of Europe; a few kilometers southeast, a Greek-Indian consortium is building the

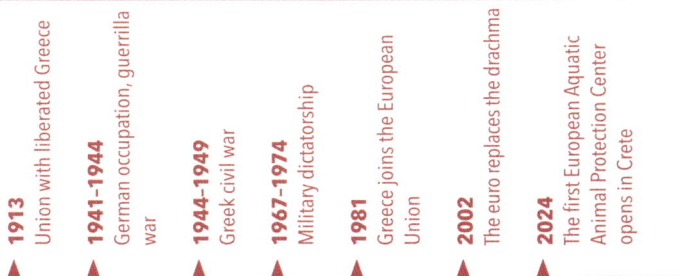

1913 Union with liberated Greece

1941–1944 German occupation, guerrilla war

1944–1949 Greek civil war

1967–1974 Military dictatorship

1981 Greece joins the European Union

2002 The euro replaces the drachma

2024 The first European Aquatic Animal Protection Center opens in Crete new airport in Iráklio; while on the south coast, Chinese investors want to build a large container ship port. On the Lassíthi Plateau, Pakistani migrant workers harvest organically grown potatoes and Cretan shepherds watch TikTok videos, or even create their own. Crete is, happily, very much a part of the globalised world.

BOTH WILD AND FRIENDLY

But Crete also has another interesting and distinctive side. Travelling from the airport, one cannot help but notice the bullet holes in the street signs which serve as target practice for many Cretans. Every shot is an expression of the locals' unease over too much state authority. This is very much an echo from their past under foreign rule: until Crete's union with Greece in 1912 and during the German occupation (1941–44) every act of resistance against the state authorities was seen as an act of bravery. To this day the Cretan motto remains: "Freedom or death!"

Despite this rather wild behaviour Crete remains one of the safest holiday destinations in the world. For centuries, hospitality has been one of their priorities, particularly so away from the tourist centres. *Rakí* and fruit are served as dessert free of charge in most tavernas and the owner often invites guests to a cup of Greek coffee. And if you should stumble on a village wedding, you may well be invited to stay and join the celebrations.

FASCINATING TOWNS AND VARIED BEACHES

Some 624,000 people live on the island and all the major towns are situated on the north coast. For visitors life is pretty laid back. Allow yourself to be beamed back 3,500 years, if only for a day, when you visit the Iráklio Archaeological Museum and the palace town of Knossós, just a few miles away. But it is not for Crete's ancient past alone that four million-plus visitors fly here every year. The main attractions are the beaches. Whether sand or shingle, the island has it all: some are miles long and some are backed with dunes. There are party beaches such as the one at Mália; tiny bays like those at Xerókambos, where no one minds how little you are wearing; beaches with rows of deck chairs and sun shades, bars and a water-sports station; and then there are more isolated strips of shingle or sand against steep cliffs and sandy slopes. None of the beaches are off-limits to visitors.

ADVENTURES FOR ACTIVE PEOPLE

Admittedly, you can find good beaches all over the world. However, there aren't many places where the mountains are as close to the sea as they are on Crete, enticing visitors away from the beach for other activities. There are over 100 unspoilt gorges to explore; stalactite caves to be discovered and 2,000m-high mountains to be climbed. And wherever you go, all the traditional mountain villages have their *kafenía*, where interested locals will be happy to greet you.

AT A GLANCE

624,000
Population

Isle of Wight: 142,000

76 PEOPLE
per km²
Isle of Wight:
372 per km²

1,066km
Coastline

Corsica: 1,000km

8,261km²
Area
Fifth largest island in the
Mediterranean

Mallorca: 3,640km²

**HIGHEST PEAK:
PSILORÍTIS**
2,456m
Ben Nevis: 1,345m

WARMEST MONTHS
JULY AND AUGUST 37°C

**MOST IMPORTANT
WORD IN GREEK**
NAI
Meaning "Yes" in
English

MOST FAMOUS CRETAN

Alexis Zorbás, hero of a novel (and subsequent movie hero – played
by Anthony Quinn) was created by Cretan author Níkos Kazantzákis

IRÁKLIO
Biggest city, with 180,000 inhabitants

**OLIVE OIL CONSUMPTION
25-30 litres per person
per year**

**PALM BEACHES?
Yes – at Vái and Préveli**

UNDERSTAND CRETE

BYZANTINE

On Crete, you'll see thousands of mostly brown signs with the English word "Byzantine" on them. The signs indicate the island's relics and remains from the Byzantine era, from around CE 500 to 1453, so roughly the time of our Middle Ages. Crete belonged to the Byzantine Empire until 1204. This empire covered all Asia Minor, the Balkans and Greece. The capital was Constantinople, renamed Istanbul after the Turks conquered it in 1453.

ANAGRAMS

Cretan signposts do not always stick to standard Greek spelling. And that can sometimes make foreigners despair. The names of many towns and villages may be spelt differently on signposts and maps, on satnavs and in Google Maps. And even more so when it comes to the Latin alphabet. "*Agia*", for instance, which means "Saint", is sometimes "*Agía*" (as used by Marco Polo), at other times it's "*Aghia*" or "Ayia". All three versions are correct. If you don't have many rules, you won't make many mistakes. All we can do is be resourceful.

PLASTICULTURE

What's that glittering over there? Many of the island's coastal plains sparkle in the sun like vast lakes when you look down on them. This is due primarily to the Netherlands. It was a Dutchman who, in the early 1960s, showed the Cretans how to grow tomatoes, fruit and vegetables in greenhouses. Thanks to the Cretan sun, there's no need for expensive heating.

Although the farmers earn good money from the *thermokípia*, all the environment gets is rubbish. That's because the greenhouses are covered in plastic film rather than glass, and once that becomes useless, it is shredded by the wind and blows away.

KRÍSIS

The word "*krísis*" ("crisis" in English) refers to the country's ongoing financial woes, and has been on every Cretan's lips since 2010. First came the economic and financial crisis, which brought tax rises, high unemployment and pension cuts in its wake. Then, in 2020, when the country was just beginning to recover, the Coronavirus hit. In 2022 Putin's troops invaded Ukraine and, suddenly, there were no more wealthy Russian tourists to bolster Crete's economy. The Cretan people have adapted to all of these events with pragmatism and good humour. Instead of spending an average of 93 minutes (statistically proven!) enjoying a coffee in the local *kafenío*, they now take a leisurely three hours. And now everyone helps out with the olive and grape harvests, rather than employing temporary eastern European labourers to do the work. This is how the locals get by with their health and their happiness intact.

STRANGE SOUNDS?

Young Cretans' taste in music is just as contemporary as that of young people in the rest of Europe. And yet, most of them are just as fascinated by *lýra* and *laoúto* as their grandparents were. The three-stringed pear-shaped lyre and the *laoúto*, a five-stringed plucked instrument, fills half of all of the music programmes on the radio, and can be heard in tavernas around the island. In fact, they even occasionally make it into the clubs.

Mostly the lyre players create a kind of monotonous speech song called *mantinádes* and *rizítika*. Although there are classics, texts are also often improvised for a specific situation or the current audience. So if you're in a taverna and everyone suddenly turns around to look at you, it's quite possible that you're currently the subject of some gentle teasing.

INSIDER TIP
Why is everybody looking at me?

SOAP OPERAS

Cretans love their favourite television programmes, mainly soaps, more and more of which are being made in Greek. Viewers demand clever and sophisticated dialogues as well as topics, issues and dramas that are relevant to Greek people. The drama crime series *I Paralía* (*The Beach*), for example, is set in the 1960s and focuses on a young doctor who, after studying in the UK, returns to Mátala, where there has been an influx of hippies. The soap *Sasmós* (*Reconciliation*) is based on a bestseller by Spyros Petroulákis about a blood feud. Such feuds still occur sporadically on Crete and, especially in the past, have caused many villages to become deserted.

CRETAN LEGENDS

Life was pretty exciting in the ancient world of the gods. One drama followed the next, and they were not always suitable for young eyes. Zeus, the father of the gods, abducted Europa, the young daughter of the Phoenician king of Crete, and fathered *Mínos*, the island's first king, with her. Mínos's wife *Pasiphae* burned with lust for a white bull. She had a life-like model of a cow made and concealed

There's no Cretan music without a *lýra*

herself inside it. The bull fell for this trick, and the queen conceived a hybrid child: the legendary minotaur.

Mínos had the beast locked up in a labyrinth, where it was regularly fed young Athenian men and virgins. The Athenian hero Theseus managed to kill the minotaur and, using Ariadne's thread, found his way out of the labyrinth. He took Ariadne home with him. But on a stopover on the island of Naxos, *Dionysos*, the god of wine and theatre, spotted the pretty Ariadne and married her. Theseus continued without her, but set black sails. These were misinterpreted by his father, the Athenian King Aegeus, who then threw himself into the sea in despair. Since then, this sea has been called the Aegean Sea.

ENTÁXI & ENTÉCHNO

When a Cretan says *entáxi*, he is saying "ok" rather than asking for a taxi. *Entéchno* is a similar trap – and as a music style, is on everyone's lips. However, it has absolutely nothing to do with techno. *Entéchno* refers to rocky ballads with Greek texts, usually performed by a soloist accompanied by a guitar. And you don't have to be a techno freak to enjoy it.

The throne room of Mínos, the purported son of Zeus, in Knossós

RARELY ALONE

Cretans don't like being alone. Even spending time with one other person is only for romantic couples, otherwise *paréa* is the order of the day. Whether they're enjoying a coffee or a meal, dancing at a nightclub or going on holiday, Cretans like to socialise in large, companionable groups. And the question that is asked later is never about the quality of the hotel or food, but whether the *paréa* was good. On the rare occasions when people do have to be alone, they still have their saints. They are always present everywhere in the form of icons. And of course, they can also be found in the many churches, chapels and on numerous painted signs on the roadsides. It means that Cretans can rest assured that they're always well protected and in good company.

SCHNAPPS AS CULTURAL HERITAGE

If you want ouzo, you're in the wrong place. People drink *rakí* on Crete, which is distilled around the clock in October and November in hundreds of tiny distilleries in villages and olive groves. It is often made without additives, only from the fermented mash that is left over after the grapes have been pressed for wine. Guesthouses, holiday apartments and hotels often offer guests a small carafe of *rakí* on arrival, and restaurants may give diners a free *rakí* with dessert, and sometimes even at breakfast.

They can afford to be generous with it, because to date the tax on the Cretan national drink, which is very

TRUE OR FALSE?

ALL CRETANS LIVE A HEALTHY LIFESTYLE

The "Cretan diet" is generally regarded as one of the healthiest. This has also translated into healthy profits for many cookbook authors on the topic. It is true that research showed a connection between diet, a long life expectancy and a low incidence of heart attacks on Crete, but this research was done in the 1950s and 60s. At that time, most people on Crete had low incomes and could only afford fruit and vegetables, plenty of (small) fish and very little meat and animal fat. Today, this has radically changed, with many overweight children on the island indicating that now there is excessive fast-food consumption and sugar intake – and less of a Spartan diet.

similar to Italian grappa, is very low. This is very much to the annoyance of the politicians in Brussels, who demand it should be taxed the same as ouzo and whisky. The Cretans are vehemently opposed to this: they consider this free use of *rakí* to be part of their cultural heritage.

WEBSITE FATIGUE

Cretan websites are often poorly maintained with little information. Rather than constantly updating their home pages, many local hoteliers have moved to social media sites instead, with almost all events now only being posted there. Smaller-scale holiday let landlords would rather pay commissions of up to 20% to booking.com and airbnb.com than use professional agencies to create and maintain their URL. More and more private businesses have accounts on Facebook, Instagram and Linkedin, too. Just type in "*crete*" or "*kriti*" and wait for the seemingly endless loading of results.

LONG HAIR & A BEARD

Orthodox priests always wear their dark gowns, even if they are out shopping with their wife and children or are just enjoying a walk. They are allowed to marry, as celibacy is only required from the rank of bishop upwards. There are three other things which every *pappás* needs: a stiff hat, long hair and a proper beard. *Pappádes* can be seen frequently, even in bars, cafés and tavernas. Their job is secure even in a crisis because they are employed by the Greek state. There is no church tax in Hellas and no issue with people leaving the Church. Almost 98 per cent of Greeks belong to the Greek Orthodox Church.

SPARTANS ON THE SKIN

Tattoos are not only popular with the many British visitors to Crete. More and more Cretans are also having images permanently applied to their skin. As they don't weigh anything, they make popular souvenirs. How about a Greek letter on your back, or a carafe of *rakí* on your arm? Ghostly

pirate ships, Spartan warriors, the philosopher Aristotle in front of the Acropolis in Athens and Greek sayings are currently among the hits at studios such as *Black Sheep* in Chaniá or *Jailhouse* in Iráklio.

NO NEED TO RUSH INTO ANYTHING

No one knows what tomorrow will bring. And the Cretans certainly don't. Nor do they make any long-term predictions. Which is why many major events and festivals – which northern Europeans usually start planning at least a year in advance – are only mentioned a few days before they take place. You'll often only find timetables and museum opening times on the Internet once they've been valid for a few days.

The Cretans even like to be a little vague when making personal arrangements. They'll arrange to meet in the morning or afternoon, evening or next week, and always add a *ta léme*: "We'll talk again". An hour before you're due to meet is still time enough to agree an exact time. Plus or minus half an hour, of course!

LOOK, THERE THEY ARE!

Vultures can be recognised by their tremendous wingspan as they circle in the sky. The roughly 300 griffon vultures on Crete have a wingspan of up to 2.60m across, while the last ten (give or take) Cretan bearded vultures measure an impressive 3m across. The best places to watch them gliding in the sky are the gorges to the west of the island. Crete's three types of eagle are even rarer than vultures: golden eagle, osprey and sea eagle. For excellent information on all these birds of prey go to *crete-birding.co.uk.*

RED EASTER EGGS

Easter is the most important holiday in the Greek-Orthodox year. It's celebrated here in accordance with the Julian calendar, so that it almost always falls on a different day to Easter in the UK. As well as spending quality time with family, Cretans are expected to attend church services at Easter. Celebratory processions take place all over Crete on the evening of Good Friday, followed by a communal Mass in church after 11pm on Easter Saturday. The services in the little harbour at Liménas, in Chersónisou and at the lake in Ágios Nikólaos are particularly noteworthy. At midnight, Christ's resurrection is celebrated with a huge firework display. On Easter Sunday, family and friends get together to feast on traditional roast lamb. Easter eggs are also a feature of the day; they are always painted bright red to symbolise the blood and suffering of Christ, on the one hand, but also the joy of his resurrection on the other.

The Eurasian griffon vulture feels at home in Crete's rocky gorges and the high skies above

EATING
SHOPPING
SPORT

Réthimno: is the Cretans' love of vibrant colours inherited from the Venetians?

EATING & DRINKING

"If I want to eat alone, I can stay at home," says almost every Cretan. And before you know it, they have drummed up friends and relations and are heading for the taverna together. Which is why you'll usually only find tables for two in the places where the tourists go.

EATING IN COMPANY

This dining community which the Cretans call paréa means that no one orders just for themselves. Instead a variety of salads and delicious starters are ordered and everyone then helps themselves. Then the large platters of fish or grilled meat are also put on the table for everyone to share. Most Cretans do without dessert, because the portions are so generous and there are usually a lot of leftovers. It is not the done thing to finish the platters and plates completely, as this would suggest that the host hasn't been generous enough.

INSIDER TIP
Do not scrape your plate!

A LITTLE BIT OF EVERYTHING

As a tourist dining out alone or with a partner, you can of course order in the normal fashion – although the Cretan way is much more fun and you get to sample a variety of dishes. By the way: it is the Cretan custom that one person usually pays for everyone; but the rise of tourism means it's now perfectly aceptable to ask for the bill to be split. In the holiday resort areas, Cretans have adapted to the customs of the holidaymakers by decorating the tavernas in the traditional way and

Moussaká always goes down well (left); a glass of water with your coffee is a must (right)

bringing the food to the table hot. A number of restaurants serve haute cuisine; their main clientele are the Cretans themselves and also Greek holidaymakers who value high-quality creative regional cuisine.

EXPENSIVE FISH

Everyone can find something to suit their tastes on Crete: from inexpensive little snack bars serving *gyros and souvláki* to upmarket Italian restaurants with Mediterranean cuisine, and from simple family tavernas with home cooking to Cretan gourmet restaurants serving exquisite creations. No matter where you eat, if you order fresh fish, be prepared to pay high prices: you will not find anything under 40 euros per kilo.

BETTER & BETTER: CRETAN WINE

When dining out, Cretans drink water and beer or wine. A wide variety of Cretan wines are available, and the quality has improved substantially in recent years. Aside from wine by the glass and the affordable rétsina – Greek white wine infused with resin from the Aleppo pine – there are also a large number of quality wines from larger or smaller cellars. Wines from the cooperative wine cellars of Sitía and Péza near Iráklio are recommended. There are also some more exclusive wines available from independent cellars, such as *Lýrarákis, Douloufákis, Económou, Manoussákis, Michalákis* and *Silva Daskaláki*.

Rakí: good with or without water

OPEN ALL HOURS

Most tavernas and restaurants are open from 9am until well after midnight. Cretans seldom eat lunch before 1pm and at night you will find them with their *paréa* dining at 10pm or even later.

SWEET TREATS

Lovers of sweet delicacies can visit a *zacharoplastío*, the Greek version of a patisserie. Here you will find a wide variety of tarts, pastries, pralines and oriental pastries such as *baklavá* and *kataifi*, which look sweeter than they actually are, and the favourite *milópita* (apple pie) which is often served with vanilla ice cream.

COFFEE CULTURE

Cretan coffee houses are where the men meet. Every village has at least one *kafenío*, most have several *kafenía*. This is necessary because each *kafenío* is usually associated with one of the three main Greek political parties: the Conservatives, the Socialists or the Communists. Although operated by a private owner, the *kafenío* is something of a public institution. There is usually no obligation to order anything. The men sit down together to talk about God and the world and above all about Greek politics or to play *távli*, draughts or cards.

When you order a coffee, remember to say exactly how you prefer it. The Cretans drink Greek coffee, which is coffee brewed together with water and sugar. *Kafé ellinikó* is served in many variations: *skétto*, without sugar; *métrio*, with some sugar; *glikó*, with lots of sugar; *dipló*, a double shot. Instant coffee is also always available. Basically you order it as *neskafé* and specify the amount of sugar you prefer. There is also the option of *neskafé sestó*, hot Nescafé, or *frappé*, cold Nescafé whisked to a foam. Cold variants of coffee like *freddo espresso* and *freddo cappuccino are also very popular* and, just like the Greek espresso, they are served with a glass of cold water.

Today's Specials

Starters

CHORIÁTIKI
A mixed Greek salad with goat's cheese and olives

FÁVA
Puréed yellow peas with onions and olive oil

KALITSÚNIA
Pastry filled with spinach (or other leafy greens) and fresh cheese

Main dishes

MOUSSAKÁ
A baked dish with minced meat, aubergines and béchamel sauce

PASTÍTSJO
Also a baked dish, made with macaroni, minced meat and béchamel sauce

STIFÁDO
Beef or rabbit stew with onions in a red sauce

JEMISTÁ
Tomatoes and peppers filled with rice, herbs and sometimes minced meat

Fish dishes

KAKAVIÁ
Fish soup similar to a bouillabaisse

SOUPIÉS GEMISTÉS
Cuttlefish mainly filled with cheese

MARÍDES
Crispy fried small fish, eaten whole

XIFÍAS
Grilled boneless swordfish steak

CHTAPÓDI
Fresh octopus served grilled, braised, or cold as a salad

Spirits

RAKÍ
Clear alcoholic pomace drink made from local grapes without any additives

OÚZO
Aniseed aperitif which becomes opaque when diluted with water

METAXÁ
The best-known Greek brandy

SHOPPING

In many of the souvenir shops in the resorts you will find lots of mass-produced goods that are seldom made in Crete. It is better to shop in the alleyways of Chaniá and Réthimno, the shops in Ágios Nikólaos, the crafters' workshops on roadsides and in the villages.

THE TASTE OF CRETE

Olives, olive oil and honey are tasty, healthy and sustainable gifts which can also be bought in Crete's numerous health food shops. Fruit preserves, dried fruit and several types of cheese are also typical of the island. A good selection of Cretan wines is available from the winemakers themselves or in specialist stores, called cáva. Rakí is sold everywhere, but ask for a tasting first because quality can vary a great deal.

MADE OF WOOD & CLAY

You will find modern and traditional ceramics all over Crete. Margarítes near Réthimno is a potters' village well worth visiting. Carvings from olive wood are particularly valuable because the wood has to be cured for a long time and is very difficult to work with. The largest selection can be found in Mátala on the southern coast. Not made of olive wood but great fun are the wooden, hand-painted bow ties and frames for sunglasses that you can buy in Iráklio.

HAND-CRAFTED JEWELLERY

In Crete you will still find some small gold- and silversmiths who produce some of their wares themselves, e.g. in Chaniá's old town and the harbour at Ágios Nikólaos. Before you buy, always check the quality. It is probably best to decline the glass of ouzo offered by the sales assistants, but you can certainly rely on the hallmarks.

Great souvenirs include leather goods (left) and premium local olive oil (right)

ANCIENT & MODERN

The museum shop in the Venetian loggia in Réthimno has the widest variety of replicas of ancient artefacts, and they also ship larger objects anywhere in the world. A few jewellers opposite the Archaeological Museum in Iráklio also sell good (but unauthorised) copies of Minoan jewellery.

LEATHER ALLEY

Chaniá is the island's leather centre. Skrídloff is a long lane that sells masses of bags and accessories "Made in Greece" (or Italy). It's not necessarily the place to find Georgína Skalídi, whose luxury bags are artistic one-offs, and available from her boutique in Chaniá or online.

IF THE SHOE FITS

When it comes to their footwear, the ladies of Crete like to strut their stuff – whether that's in high heels, sandals or boots. At family-run Legáki (Odós Katecháki/Moní Odigítrias | legaki shoes.gr) in Iráklio, handmade, everyday – but pretty – sandals and shoes are sold at good prices.

INSIDER TIP
Be nice to your feet

FASHION

Cretan fashionistas fly to Athens for their shopping; internationally renowned labels, plus popular brands such as Zara and H&M, can only be found in Iráklio town centre. High-quality T-shirts and children's clothing made in Crete are available from Ágios Nikólaos.

CRETAN SOUNDS

Whether it is traditional Cretan lýra sounds or the rock music of the Greek charts – you will find them in any music shop in Crete.

SPORT & ACTIVITIES

The mountains and sea are the island's sports arenas. Daredevils try their luck on Europe's second-highest bungee jump; the more cautious venture out for some yoga on an SUP board. Some like to attach themselves to a parachute and be pulled over the water, while cyclists can choose between mountain bikes, racing bikes and e-bikes.

BUNGEE JUMPING
A bungee jump at Arádena, near the south coast, takes bravery. You can dive 138m from the bridge into the Arádena Gorge: *Liquidbungy (July–Aug Sat/Sun noon–5pm | 100 euros | Arádena | tel. 69 37 61 51 91 | bungy.gr).*

CANYONING & CLIMBING
You can find numerous guided canyoning and climbing tours at *cretan adventures.gr*, while information for self-guided climbing can be found at *climbincrete.com. Kóstas Marmatzákis (Odós Evrópis 22, Iráklio | tel. 69 47 01 65 32 | peripetia365.gr)*, a former professional climber who speaks good English and French, runs climbing tours for up to six people. He has created many of the routes himself, and also offers a tour that includes Crete's only Via Ferrata in his program; and he has plans to create a Via Cordata. His favourite areas are near Iráklio and in the Asteroúsia Mountains.

DIVING
Cretan diving sites are particularly suited to beginners due to their crystal-clear water, good centres and interesting underwater rock formations. However, there are few fish to be seen. In Crete archaeologists also have a say in the approval of dive sites as they fear that divers will disturb excavations and even smuggle pieces out of the country.

Diving schools include: *Atlantis Diving Centre (Beach Hotel, Ádele)* and in the *Club Marine Palace Hotel (Panórmo | tel. 28 31 07 16 40 | atlantis-creta.com); Creta Maris Dive Center (Liménas Chersónisou | Hotel Creta Maris | tel. 28 97 02 21 22 | dive-cretamaris.gr); Dive Together (on the coastal road, Plakiás | tel. 28 32 03 23 13 | dive2gether.com); Notos Mare (at the new harbour, Chóra Sfakíon | tel. 28 21 00 85 36 | notos mare.com). Some also offer introductory courses for adults and for children.*

HIKING

The E4 European long-distance hiking trail stretches from the west to the east coast of Crete. You should allow at least four weeks for the complete hike. The signposting is good but not perfect. Fitness is essential because you will be crossing mountains, and a tent is also useful. Particularly popular and easy to manage for experienced mountain hikers on holiday are the four sections of the route between Paleochóra and Chóra Sfakíon, totalling approx. 60km. If you lose interest mid-way, you can board the coastal steamer to continue your journey.

If you prefer guided hikes, you can book with one of the many local operators, such as *alternativecrete.com, cretatrekking.com* or *hiking-crete.com.*

HORSE RIDING

Riding stables for experienced riders are at *Odysseia Stables (tel. 28 97 05 10 80, 69 42 83 60 83 | horseriding.gr)* in Avdoú en route to the Lassíthi Plateau. Both offer accommodation nearby. Guided hacks for absolute beginners are available from stables in and around *Liménas Chersónisou.*

MOUNTAIN BIKING

Crete is an ideal destination for mountain bikers. There are lots of good biking centres that offer a range of tour packages for all levels of difficulty. Those who prefer to take it easy can take a support van up to the starting point and then cycle downhill, while ambitious bikers can challenge themselves cycling between mountain peaks. Organisers offer day trips (*approx. 45–90 euros, children 25–40 euros*) and week packages. E-bikes are generally available too.

Good agencies are *Freak Mountainbike Centre (tel. 69 85 81 02 40 | freak-mountainbike.com)* in Palékastro; *Hellas Bike (main road opposite the Bank of Cyprus | tel. 28 21 06 08 58 | hellasbike.net)* in Agía Marína near Chaniá; *Kreta Bike (Odós Nikéas 48 | tel. 28 31 07 23 83 | kretabike.com)* on the road between Réthimno and Ádele and the Arkádi Monastery; and *Anso Travel (tel. 28 32 03 14 44 | ansotravel.com)* in Plakiás on the south coast.

There are five centres affiliated to *Crete Cycling (crete-cycling.com)* in Ágios Nikólaos, Móchlos, Palékastro and Iráklio (all year), and Agía Galíni (which also has racing bikes). A good bike costs 20–35 euros a day or 120–150 euros per week.

INSIDER TIP
Up for a challenge?
Challenging day trips on e-mountain bikes in very small groups are arranged by Adam Frogákis *(tel. 69 44 74 06 93 | cretactiv.com)* in central and southern Crete. In addition to day trips, you can also book multi-day tours.

RUNNING

Marathons are held on Crete several times a year. These events also allow runners to cover shorter distances such as 5km or 10km. In June, a 35km race starts on the Nída mountain plateau and leads up to the peak of Mount Psilorítis. You can find information about the *Crete Marathon* on *cretemarathon.gr,* and about the half marathon on *cretehm.com.*

SEA KAYAKING

On the west coast, *Fit in Crete (Kissamos | tel. 69 99 44 63 84 | fitincrete.com* offers both one-day and multi-day tours using sit-on kayaks.

SKIING

Yes, you did read that right – and we're not talking about waterskiing in the

Riding on the beach near Liménas Chersónisou

summer, but about alpine skiing between Christmas and March. There are no groomed slopes or ski centres, but there is plenty of untouched deep snow on the three high mountains of the island. Dates and routes must be agreed upon depending on the weather, and you can rent equipment – except for shoes. You definitely need a guide who can also arrange transfers. *Kóstas Marmatzákis (tel. 69 47 01 65 32 | peripetia365.gr)* has a lot of experience, and you can discuss your plans with him in English. If there is enough snow, he is happy to cross all three of the island's high mountains on skis within a week.

WATER SPORTS

Almost all the popular beaches offer water-sports options, from water skiing to jet skiing and parasailing. Paddle boats and canoes can also be hired in front of the larger hotels and surfboards are available on many of the beaches, mainly on the north and east coast. Good windsurfing schools can be found at the larger centres such as *Freak Station (tel. 69 79 25 38 61 | freak-surf.com)* on *Koureménos Beach* in Palékastro, who also specialise in kite surfing.

The specialist in stand-up paddling (SUP) is the Cretan *Stéfanos Averkiou (Maráthi Bay, Sosorídes Beach | tel. 69 36 07 27 30 | supincrete.com)*, who can be found on the Akrotíri Peninsula near Chaniá. His offer includes hire, courses and guided day trips, and yoga on a paddleboard is his speciality.

HOLIDAY PLANNER

K r i t i k o

RÉTHIMNO P. 58
Beaches, villages, monasteries, caves and minarets

Old Town ★

Kísamos/ Kastélli

Chaniá

Vámos

Venetian Harbour ★

Réthimno

Perama

Feel at peace ✓

Discover Cretan cuisine ✓

Discover Cretan cuisine ✓

Elafonísi Beach ★

Arkádi Monastery ★

Descend into the underworld ✓

Paleohora

Préveli ★

Mires

CHANIÁ P. 40
Old town by the sea, dream-like South Sea lagoons, wild gorges

Mátala ★

L i v i k o

20 km
12.43 mi

Pelagos

IRÁKLIO p. 74
Bustling big city, Minoan palaces and a vivid nightlife scene

ÁGIOS NIKÓLAOS p. 94
Picturesque small town, green mountain valleys and an island with a disturbing history

Archaeological Museum ★

✔ Feel the earth move

Dance till you drop ✔

Party in traditional Cretan style ✔

Iráklio

Knossós

✔ Discover Cretan cuisine

Spinalónga ★

Ágios ✔ Captain your own boat

Nikólaos

Lassíthi Plateau ★

Sitía

Fresh fish and a sea view – that's it! ✔

Ierápetra

Pirgos

IERÁPETRA p. 108
A touch of Africa, two islets and few tourists

Take a boat to the beach ✔

SITÍA p. 118
Perfect tranquillity, a palm beach, an oleander valley and remote coves

Pelagos

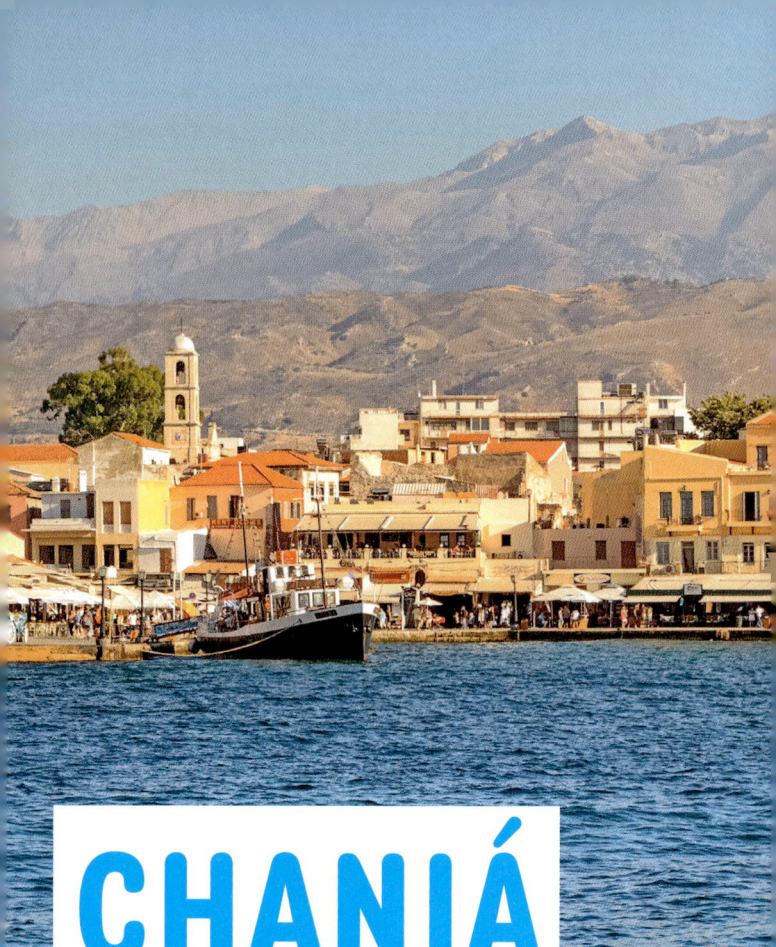

CHANIÁ

Born to be wild? Then Chaniá in western Crete is the perfect holiday region for you. The White Mountains contain almost more gorges than villages, while between the rough cliff faces of the Libyan Sea are isolated beaches and only a few tiny villages.

Some of these villages can only be reached by boat. In the lagoons in the extreme west, you'll swim in turquoise waters reminiscent of the South Seas, while in the protected valleys you can pick oranges straight from the trees. Sheep graze between ancient ruins, while the

A perfect catwalk – Chaniá's harbour promenade

Middle Ages surround you in the old town of Chaniá. You won't find many of the bathing resorts in this part of the island advertised in holiday brochures – these ones are mostly for independent travellers.

Chaniá (pop. 111,000) is the main city in the region and the most beautiful of Crete's towns. Boredom is unheard of in the island's second-largest town. Hotels and guesthouses often have a roof garden, from where you can see the vast Aegean and the almost 2,500m-high mountain peaks.

CHANIÁ

MARCO POLO BUCKET LIST

1 ✓ Discover Cretan cuisine

Learn the secrets of Cretan cuisine on a cookery course at *Vamos Traditional Village*, for example ➤ p. 51

2 ✓ Feel at peace

Enjoy the solitude at *Polirrinía Acropolis*, where the ruins are set in a beautiful natural landscape ➤ p. 52

10 ✓ Conquer a legendary gorge

Hike through Crete's most famous gorge and complete one of Greece's most popular walking routes ➤ p. 55 and p. 146

If you don't want to join the queues of cars making their way to Bálos Beach, then hop aboard one of the small boats that leave from Falássarna and Kíssamos instead.

Chaniá and the resorts to the west are perfect for a holiday that combines town and beach. You can easily shuttle between the two by bus.

9 Bálos Beach ★

Gramvoúsa

Ροδωπός
Rodopós

Κολυμβάρι
Kolimbari

Καλυδονία
Kalydonia

Μάλεμε
Máleme

Καλυβιανή
Kaliviani

Δραπανιάς
Drapanias

90

Falássarna **8**

Kíssamos **7**

For several years now, Chaniá Bay has been known throughout Greece for its chic beach bars.

Incurable romantics should stay on at Falássarna Beach until sunset to watch the blazing red sun sink into the sea.

Ποταμίδα
Potamida

6 Polirrínia

2 ✓

Βατόλακκος
Vatolakkos

Sfinári **10**

Μελίσσια
Melissia

Τοπόλια
Topolia

41 km, 1 hr 10 mins

Σηρικάρι
Sirikari

Πλαγιά
Plaghia

Κεφαλή
Kefali

Βλάτος
Vlatos

Μυλωνες
Milones

Πρασές
Prases

Αμυγδαλοκεφάλι
Amigdhalokefali

Έλος
Elos

Χρυσοσκαλίτισσα
Chrisoskalitissa

Πλεμενιανά
Plemeniana

13 Iríni Gorge

Επανωχώρι
Epanochori

Καλλιθέα
Kallithea

Λαγκαδάς
Lagkadas

Ροδοβάνι
Rodovani

Μονή
Moni

11 Elafonísi Beach ★

Άνυδροι
Anydri

14 Soúgia

12 Paleochóra

Livikó

Pélagos

Travel by bus to either Soúgia or Chóra Sfakíon and then hire a boat to explore the southern coast. You could visit a different village or beach each day.

6 km
3.73 mi

Σταυρός
Stavros

Ακρωτήρι
Akrotíri

Καμπάνι
Kampani

1 Akrotíri Peninsula ★

Αγία Μαρίνα
Agía Marína

Harbour ★

Καθιανά
Kathiana

Στέρνες
Sternes

● **Chaniá**
p. 44

Γαλατάς
Galatas

Old Town ★

Σούδα
Souda

Kritikó

Pélagos

Όαση
Oasi

A90

90

Κόκκινο Χωριό
Kokkino Chorio

2 Áptera

Καλύβες
Kalyves

5 Fournés

Σκινές
Skines

Νέο Χωριό
Neo Chorio

Δράπανος
Drapanos

Μεσκλά
Meskla

Vámos **3** **1** ✓

Κεφαλάς
Kefalás

In the summer, daily buses run from Chaniá to the region's most popular beaches. This means you don't need a hire car to reach Falássarna, Bálos (bus to Kíssamos, then boat) or even Elafonísi.

Νίπος
Nipos

Βρύσες
Vrises

90 **4** Georgioúpoli

CRETE
KPHTH

Βαφές
Vafes

Αλίκαμπος
Alikambos

Δράμια
Dramia

47 km, 4 hrs

Αμουδάρι
Amoudari

10 ✓ **15** Samariá Gorge ★

Ίμβρος
Imbros

Αγία Ρουμέλη
Agia Roumeli

Άγιος Ιωάννης
Agios Ioannis

Ανώπολη
Anopoli

16 Ímbros Gorge

Πατσιανός
Patsianos

18 Loutró

17 Chóra Sfakíon

20 km, 1 hr

Órthi Ámmos Beach

19 Frangokastéllo

CHANIÁ TOWN

(🔖 D–E2) **The regional capital, Chaniá, is worth a few days of your holiday; of all the Cretan towns, it is the beauty queen. And it has a lot to offer visitors.**

A good programme would start with museums and plenty of maritime touches in the morning; enjoy lunch in the harbour and some downtime in the hammam. Then do some relaxed, exclusive shopping, followed by din-

which was shaped by the Venetians. The new town has little to offer apart from the entertaining City Park.

SIGHTSEEING

ÁGIOS NIKÓLAOS CHURCH

You won't see this anywhere else: a church with a minaret! When the Turks conquered Crete in 1669, they converted many of the Christian churches into Islamic places of prayer. All they had to do was remove the icons, paint over or scrape off the murals, install a prayer recess facing Mecca, and place a minaret on top. After 1913, these

The Maritime Museum celebrates Crete's seafaring history

ner in the old Turkish baths and a carriage ride. The evening can continue with some traditional lyre music and, later on, jazz until sunrise. You won't have to leave the ⭐ *old town*,

mosques were turned back into churches. All the other minarets were removed, but this one was eventually restored. *Platía 1821*

ARCHAEOLOGICAL MUSEUM

This museum moved from its previous home in a Gothic church to the Chalépa district in 2022, and is a masterpiece of modern architecture. The most interesting things in it are the primitive hunting scenes on sarcophagi that are over 3,300 years old. A tiny seal from the 15th century BCE is unique, and can also be seen on the museum's (free) brochure; it is of a monumental lance-bearer on the rooftops of Minoan Chaniá. *April–Oct Wed–Mon 8am–8pm, Nov–March Wed–Mon 8.30am–3.30pm | admission 6 euros | Odós Chalidón 25 | ⊙ 30–45 mins*

CITY PARK 👪

Few tourists visit Chaniá's "green lung". Local Chanioti sit in the chicest, most traditional coffee house on the island, *O Kípos (daily from 8am | €€)*, playing cards, *távli*, Scrabble and Monopoly as they drink their *cafés ellinikós* or a glass of champagne. A few steps further on, Cretan wild goats with their mighty horns graze quietly, while in the evenings, films are shown

in the summer cinema under the starry sky. *Odós Dimokratías/Odós Tzanakáki*

FOLKLORE MUSEUM

If you think museums are dead, then try this one. You'll see craftsmen sitting in their historic workshops, while a vintner distills *rakí* all year round, and a grandmother shivers by the fire even in summer. The fact that they are all made of wax has the advantage that your photos will be nice and clear. *Daily 10am–5pm | admission 3 euros | Odós Chalidón 46b | ⊙ 30–45 mins*

HARBOUR ⭐

A blessing in disguise: because the harbour in Chaniá is so silted up, the only boats that can enter are fishing boats and yachts. This means that the long harbour quay is almost traffic-free, which makes it perfect for a stroll. The only vehicles on the tarmac are horse-drawn carriages. Cafés and tavernas nestle cheek by jowl between the *Maritime Museum* and the eye-catching but ugly *Mosque of the Janissaries*. After that, the quayside gets quieter as you pass more or less preserved Venetian shipyards and a few basic fish restaurants before reaching the *Minoan Ship* and the night-time party quarter on the east side of the harbour. You can walk or jog along the 500m-long jetty that stretches westwards.

JEWISH QUARTER

Narrow streets, tiny shops, cosy tavernas: the *Odós Kondiláki* is worth a visit. The town's Jewish community lived here until the Holocaust. All that remains of it is the tiny *Etz Hayyim synagogue (Mon–Thu 10am–6pm, Fri 10am–3pm, Nov–April Mon–Thu 10am–5pm, Fri 10am–3pm | Párodos Kon diláki | etz-hayyim-hania.org)*, which was a Christian church until 1669. International voluntary guides are available to take you around (for a donation of 2 euros) and will tell you about what happens in a synagogue.

MARITIME MUSEUM
How lovely that models exist. This shipping museum shows us what the town looked like in the year 1600. History lovers in particular will appreciate the retelling of the historic sea battles with miniature ships; you can even have a close look at a Venetian galley ship. On the top floor, Germans and Austrians are confronted by a dark chapter in their history: the attack on Crete in 1941. *Mon–Sat 9am–4pm, in winter 9am–3.30pm | admission 4 euros | Aktí Kundurióti | mar-mus-crete.gr | ⊙ 30–45 mins*

MINOAN SHIP
Would you row from Crete to Piraeus? A Cretan team attempted it in 2004 and, despite the auxiliary sails, it took them 27 days to sail the 390km. What made it even more amazing is that the bold men and women were travelling in the same kind of boat as the Minoans would have used for their long-distance sailing expeditions over 3,300 years before. Today, this scientifically based reproduction is housed in an old Venetian shipyard, where video films tell you more about the construction and trip of the *Minoan Ship. May–Oct Mon–Sat 9.20am–4pm | admission 3 euros | Odós Defkalónia | ⊙ 20 mins*

TOPANÁS
Oh, sweet seduction! You'll struggle to resist the plethora of tiny shops and artists' studios that have opened up in the old district of Topanás.

Quality and originality abound on straight-as-a-die Odós Theotokópoulou and its side streets, and if you climb up the *Schiávo bastion* you'll be able to see over the old town to the sea.

EATING & DRINKING

BOHÈME
It's just ten metres from the main thoroughfare, but sitting here is like being on another planet – one that is idyllic and calm. Brunch and cocktails are served at all times of the day and night, so sit back and allow the outside world to disappear. *Daily 9.30am–2am | Odós Chalidón 26 | boheme-chania.gr | €€*

SECRET TASTES
Hunger pangs but not much money? Then you've come to the right place. This mini-taverna has four tables on the pavement out front and seven inside. The young chef and waiter are ambitious and keen to convince the local clientele to sample more modern variations on traditional cuisine. Anything you can't eat is packed up for you to take away. *Mon–Sat 1pm–midnight | Odós Kóraka 24 | €*

CHANIÁ TOWN

200 m
219 yd

Kolpos Hanion

Minoan Ship

To Stáchi

Maritime Museum

Kallergon

Topanás   Carmela

Harbour ★

Fagotto

Al Hamam

Akti Kanari

Adéspoto

Ágios Nikólaos Church

Meletiou

Bohème

atriarchou Ioanníkeiou

Jewish Quarter

Folklore
Museum

Georgína Skalídi

Metaxaki

Archaeological
Museum

Chalidon

Tsouderon

Ελ. Βενιζέλου   El. Venizelou

Municipal Market

Selinou

Old town ★

Secret
Tastes

Andrea Papandreou

Plastira
Πλαστήρα

Tzanakaki

Kissamos

Kυδωνίας   Kydonias

Plastira

City Park

Aπoκoρώνου

Tζανακάκη

Aπoλoγιαννoú

TO STÁCHI

Stélios is a Cretan pioneer of vegetarian and vegan cuisine. In his small tavern he magics delightful morsels from vegetables and salad, using aromatic herbs, orange zest and other flavours. His white house wine is one of the best on the island. *Mon–Sat 1–10pm | Odós Epimenídou | €–€€*

SHOPPING

CARMELA

In this tiny shop run by Carmela and Dimitri Iatrópoulou you'll have all the time in the world to look around in peace. No single item of jewellery or pottery is repeated, and everything was made either by the owners themselves or by their Greek friends. Allow Carmela to recommend the right gemstone to match your skin tone and bank balance. *Odós Angélu 7*

GEORGÍNA SKALÍDI

INSIDER TIP
Out of the ordinary

Do you find symmetry boring? Post-modern clutch-bags are this designer's passion, and she designs them all herself in coloured leather. A recent addition to her range includes brilliant costume jewellery, which is surprisingly affordable. *Mon–Sat 11am–2pm, Tue, Thu, Fri also 6–9pm, Sun 7–10pm | Odós Chatzimicháli Dalagiánni 58 | georginaskalidi.com*

MUNICIPAL MARKET

Until recently, this century-old building was home to souvenir sellers mixed in with the greengrocers and fishmongers and quaint tavernas. In 2022, it was cleared for major renovation works, and is expected to open in renewed splendour in 2025. *Platía Venizélos*

SPORT & ACTIVITIES

There are always some drivers with their one-horse carriages waiting for customers by the harbour. Tours around the old town last 25 or 50 minutes and cost 30 or 50 euros respectively. The best times are at dusk and in the early evening, with departures from the Mosque of the Janissaries/Yali Mosque.

For a more active exploration of Chaniá during the day or at night, rent a *segway (30–85 euros / 60–180 mins | Odós Ep. Chrisánthou 25 | tel. 69 44 59 71 59 | chaniasegwaytours.com).*

Regular bus services to the large *Aqua Creta Limnoúpolis* water park *(limnoupolis.gr)* depart from Platía 1866.

A different perspective: segway over the city's cobblestones

BEACHES

The most beautiful beaches accessible by bus (line 21) are to the west of Chaniá. 🎭 *Agíon Apostólon Beach* is particularly suitable for children, and is fairly undeveloped except for a beach bar under ancient trees.

WELLNESS

AL HAMAM

The most original and also the smallest of all wellness oases on the island is at Chaniá harbour. It has an old-world atmosphere, but is actually high-tech. Step onto the roof and drink your Turkish tea from one of the typical small glasses. You will almost feel as if you are in a sultan's palace. *Daily 11am–10pm | from 25 euros/ 45 mins | Pl. El. Venizélou 14 | tel. 28 21 05 90 05 | alhammam.gr*

INSIDER TIP
Oriental flavours

NIGHTLIFE

There's plenty going on in the old town all year round. The standard discos, beloved of the happy-drinker tourists, are just behind the Mosque of the Janissaries in the harbour on the short Odós Sourméli. The *Klik Bar* is always popular. The local in-crowd prefers to meet in the music clubs on the eastern side of the harbour, behind the striking Hotel Porto Veneziano. For those with slightly different tastes in music, there's a jazz club and numerous tavernas with Cretan lyre performances.

ADÉSPOTO ⚑

This live music venue is located in a house in the old town which lost its roof in 1940. It means you can enjoy Cretan and Greek music played under a starry sky. *Mon–Sat noon–1am | Odós Sifáka/Ecke Odós Melchisedek | adespotochania.gr | €€*

FAGOTTO

If you'd rather leave the dancing to others and prefer instead to enjoy good, solid jazz and rock in a cosy bar or down a narrow street in the old town, then the relaxed, well-established Fagotto is your musical home from home. *Daily 9pm–3am | Odós Ángelou 16*

AROUND CHANIÁ

1 AKROTÍRI PENINSULA ⭐

50–60km round trip / approx. 3 hrs from Chaniá by car, 5½ hrs incl. hike

You'll be caught between monasteries and military cannons here: tax-payers' money goes up in smoke at NATO's rocket-launch site on the peninsula, while the monks in two monasteries pray for peace. And although you can only see the military barracks from a distance, you are welcome to visit the monasteries. The monks at *Agía Triáda (daily from 8am–7pm | admission 2.50 euros)* work busily producing olive oil, wine and schnapps. You can also visit the wine cellar with the adjoining tasting room and the

In Áptera you can picnic between ancient relics and the remains of a monastery

17th-century church with its traditional murals.

Prayer and the lovely garden are the main interests of the extremely devout monks at the 16th-century *Gouvernéto Monastery (Sun 5am–noon and 5–8pm, Oct–Easter 4–7pm; Mon, Tue, Thu, Sat 10am–noon and 5–7pm | admission free)*, which strongly resembles a desert fort. Modest clothing is essential here. Fancy a little walk? A paved path from the Gouvernéto Monastery leads through the quiet landscape past a chapel in a stalactite cave to the now-abandoned *Katholikó Monastery* beside a gorge. ▢ *E–F2*

2 ÁPTERA

16km / 25 mins from Chaniá by car
Romantic ruins will draw you to the rocky plateau near the coast. In early spring, you'll share the tiers of the ancient theatre with scarlet poppies. The backdrop of the White Mountains against green valleys also merits a round of applause. **INSIDER TIP** **Hearing test** Check out your echo in one of the two vast Roman cisterns, then unpack your picnic in the courtyard of a medieval abbey. The attendant limits his activities to selling tickets at the ticket desk, so you're free to explore as you wish *(Wed–Mon April–Oct 8am–8pm, Nov–March 8.30am–3.30pm | admission 4 euros | ancientaptera.gr)*.

As you continue on the short drive to the Ottoman fort on the escarpment of the plateau, you'll come across the remains of the once kilometre-long town wall and will pass fields of giant fennel, which the earlier fishermen and sailors used as fire lighters. Break

on the Apokóronas peninsula had the idea of restoring empty old houses and renting them out. Above an old cistern on the main street is the taverna *Stérna tou Bloumósifis (Mon–Thu from 5pm, Fri–Sun from 1pm | €€)*, which serves creative Cretan cuisine. 📖 *F3*

4 GEORGIOÚPOLI

40km / 40 mins from Chaniá by car

The mix is right: Georgioúpoli is a typical Cretan village with a perfectly good life of its own, and yet it is perfectly prepared for holidaymakers as well. Fishermen still bring their catches to the river harbour in the mornings. Pedalos and kayaks are for hire right under the bridge; you can take them up the river and watch the turtles. Grannies, grandpas and nursing mums settle down on the modern *platía* to watch the tourists.

A 14km sandy beach starts just to the east of the harbour. Public buses go to nearby Réthimno and to Chaniá at least every hour, while there are lots of quiet villages in the surrounding area that offer pure rusticity.

🎭 *Fun trains* take tourists into the surrounding countryside. At night, *Café Titos* on the *platía* and the *Beach Bar Tropicana* become clubs.

Lake Kournás, which is just 3km away and easy to get to, is the largest mountain lake on the island, and offers a beach, tavernas and pedal-boat hire. In the mountain village of *Kournás*, 🎭 donkey whisperer Arno de Vrij *(Sat/Sun 10am | mandali-kournas.com)* offers two-hour walks with his four-legged friends. 📖 *F3–4*

open one of the dried stalks (which grow to lengths of up to 2m) in late summer or autumn, and you can make the pulp in them glow – just hold a cigarette lighter or match to it, blow for a few seconds, and you'll have a glimmer. And that is exactly how Prometheus first brought fire to mankind on earth. 📖 *E3*

3 VÁMOS

22km / 40 mins from Chaniá by car

If gentle tourism is your thing, then rent a village house in Vámos (pop. 700) through *Vamos Traditional Village (tel. 28 25 02 21 90 | vamosvillage.gr | €€–€€€)*. You'll quickly become part of the community and find yourself sitting among the locals on the *platía* and 🔵 taking Cretan cooking lessons in a former olive press. In 1995, a group of young people in the large main town

5 FOURNÉS

15km / 25 mins from Chaniá by car

Could it be any healthier! The restaurant of the 50-acre ✿ *Botanical Park of Crete (March–mid-Nov daily from 9am until 75 mins before sunset | admission 7 euros | on the road to Ómalos | botanical-park.com | €€)* serves freshly squeezed juices from fruit they have harvested themselves. And you can rest assured we're not just talking about the oranges that grow on tens of thousands of trees here in Fournés and the surrounding villages, but also about more exotic varieties such as papaya, guava, passionfruit and kiwi.

The kitchen prepares typical Cretan dishes flavoured with local herbs, lime and lemongrass, and bakes its own bread in the wood-fired oven.

Not hungry? Then go for a walk along the 3km of trails through the Mediterranean and tropical gardens, and we'll talk again. ▢ *D3*

6 POLIRRINÍA ✓

53km / 75 mins from Chaniá by car

Alone at last! It's unusual to see strangers in this tiny mountain village, which 2,500 years ago was an important town. Your best choice is to follow the small signpost to the Acropolis. At the point where the road ends between the walls of the old houses is the medieval church *Ágii Patéres*, with lots of old inscriptions on its exterior walls. They were originally part of a temple, and you can still see the stone blocks used for the supporting walls on the edge of the churchyard, as well as an old circular threshing floor. A

15-minute walk along the narrow footpath will take you through the maquis and up a rocky hill with ancient walls along the slopes. <mark>The tiny chapel is the perfect place for a picnic in complete isolation.</mark> ▢ *B3*

INSIDER TIP
Heavenly shade

7 KÍSSAMOS

42km / 40 mins from Chaniá by car

Far from the mainstream, you're now in Crete's westernmost little town in the sun. For most visitors to Crete, Kíssamos (pop. 4,300) is merely the starting point for the boat trip to *Bálos Beach* (see p. 53). The only tourist attraction as such is the approximately 150m-long beach promenade with cafés and tavernas including the *Kelári (€€)*. West of that is a good sandy beach, while to the east is a 1km-long shingle beach. Opposite the *Archaeological Museum (Wed–Mon 8am–3.30pm | admission 4 euros | Platía Tzanakáki),* with its lovely mosaic floors, is the *Strata Tours (Platía Tzanakáki | tel. 28 22 02 42 49 | stratatours.com)* travel agency, which hires out bicycles. Owner Stélios goes hiking with visitors, and will even take you into some of the houses in the villages. ▢ *A2*

8 FALÁSSARNA

53km / 55 mins from Chaniá by car

From November to April tomatoes are grown in countless greenhouses on the coastal plain, but during the summer months, sandy beaches and a scattering of tavernas and small hotels entice independent travellers to

Falássarna. *Falássarna Activities (falassarnaactivities.gr)* at "Big Beach" rents out SUPs, canoes and jet skis. Added historical interest comes from the excavation of the ancient fortified harbour, complete with quay wall and mooring stones, although the archaeological site is often closed to visitors. 📖 *A2*

🟦9 BÁLOS BEACH ⭐ 🦇

52km / 75 mins from Chaniá by car (to the car park) or 80 mins from Kíssamos by boat

Wow! Whether you come on the excursion boat from Kíssamos or on foot from the car park at the end of a rough track, the views of the lagoon of *Bálos* with its white beaches against the bare cliffs will bowl you over. And apart from a single (overpriced) taverna, there are no buildings in sight.

Sailors can explore the island of *Gramvoúsa* with its Venetian fort on the way over. While car users and hikers can ride a donkey down from the car park to the beach.

Travel here along a 7km track that is suitable (with care!) for cars *(toll 2 euros)* from the village of Kaliviani. Small boats from Falássarna run trips here *(40 euros | falassarnacruise.gr)*, while larger boats from Kíssamos are offered by *Cretan Daily Cruises (28 euros | cretandailycruises.com)*. 📖 *A2*

🟦10 SFINÁRI

57km / 75 mins from Chaniá by car

Hidden between the tourist hotspots of Bálos and Elafonísi is this unspoilt gem, a throwback to a less commercial era on the island. During the week, you can lie on the near-deserted beach and dine under ancient tamarisk trees in peace. There are also a handful of tavernas where you can camp for free. On the main road is *Taverna O*

Looking even more beautiful from a distance: the lagoon of Bálos

Hiking the Samariá Gorge

Georgákas (daily from 9am | €), which has locally caught game and fish on the menu. 🔲 *A3*

🔟 ELAFONÍSI BEACH ⭐ 🌴
78km / 2 hrs from Chaniá by car
Blue, turquoise or green? The shallow waters on the finest sand shimmer on this beach in every imaginable hue. This has made the beach extremely popular with visitors, especially in high summer. Tavernas and guest-houses, along with the car park, have been banished to the hinterland. So nature comes into its own. Those who would like to have Elafonísi mostly to themselves should stay here or in the neighbouring village

of Chrissoskalítissa, where the epony-mous, blindingly white monastery can also be seen in a highly photogenic position on a rock. 🔲 *A4*

🔢 PALEOCHÓRA
71km / 80 mins from Chaniá by car
It doesn't get any warmer than this! The large village on the south coast is the warmest place in the whole of Greece. Farmers take advantage of this for the countless solar-heated greenhouses all over the coastal plain. And tourists like it because they can sit outside all night even in spring and autumn. The community and hosts are happy to play along. Every day at 7pm, the main street turns into a long *Food Court,* with tavernas, cafés and bars. Just a few steps, and you'll be in the garden of the island's first wine bar, *Monika's Garden (daily from 6pm | on the road from the main junction to the sandy beach | €€)*, or you can watch classic films and the latest blockbusters at the *Summer Cinema*.

There is a long, extra-wide sandy beach on one side of the peninsula with the village. The other side will be for people who prefer to lie on shin-gle. All sorts of boat trips start in the tiny harbour, while quiet mountain villages in the region are good desti-nations for hikers. The only historical sight in the village is the freely accessi-ble Venetian castle complex *Kástro Sélino,* which has one main purpose: people meet here at sunset. Night owls usually experience the sunrise at *Ágios Bar* on the main junction in the village. There's plenty of time to go to bed after that. 🔲 *B5*

13 IRÍNI GORGE

43km / 1 hr from Chaniá by car

The Iríni Gorge is just as impressive as the Samariá Gorge but not as well known. The rock faces soar hundreds of metres high; many parts of the gorge are covered in forest and huge boulders lie in the summer-dry river bed. The hike starts at the southern edge of the village of *Agía Iríni* on the road from Chaniá to Soúgia. A small forest restaurant is at the entrance. The gorge ends after 7km at the simple little *Taverna Oásis (€),* which fits in perfectly with the landscape. The selection is limited but the food is authentic. Here you are also welcome to eat your picnic, provided that you order the drinks, such as hot mountain tea. From here a road continues for 5km to Soúgia *(taxi booking tel. 69 40 85 98 60 or tel. 69 70 34 44 22).* 📖 *C4*

INSIDER TIP
Bring your own food

14 SOÚGIA

60km / 90 mins from Chaniá by car

There isn't much to say about Soúgia, which is precisely why regulars keep returning there every year. There are no other towns or villages as far as the eye can see; nothing worth visiting, no "you've-simply-got-to-see-this" pressures. With a crystal-clear conscience, you can focus entirely on enjoying the long shingle beach, the mix of Cretan and Alsatian cuisine served at the *Ómikron (€€),* meet other Soúgia fans at the *Lotos Music Café* next door, and perhaps agree to share a sea taxi with them to a nearby beach. 📖 *C4*

15 SAMARIÁ GORGE ⭐ ✔

37km / 1 hr from Chaniá towards Omalos (by bus), and then on foot or by shuttlebus to the gorge entrance

Crete's most famous gorge is the location of one of Greece's most popular walking routes. If you're fit enough to undertake this challenging hike, you'll be rewarded with fascinating natural scenery. The route climbs over 1,250m, leading you between dramatic cliffs, over rubble and across footbridges to an abandoned village, past pine trees, cypresses and intriguing rock formations. Always stick to the main path for your own safety and to protect the natural environment – even if you spot one of Crete's wild goats and are tempted to take a close-up photo! For details, see p. 146. 📖 *C4*

see p. 146

16 ÍMBROS GORGE

55km / 1 hr from Chaniá by car

Glutton for punishment or slacker? If you think hiking through the

THE RIGHT TO BEAR ARMS

Road signs are used as shooting targets by some Cretans – you'll see the pockmarks on signs all over the island. Hitting a "Stop" or a "No parking" sign is considered proof of a Cretan's love of freedom and disdain for authority. According to statistics, every male islander owns at least one firearm, but violent crimes are rare on the island. Instead, the guns are fired for joy, at weddings and baptisms, for example.

Plenty of sea and peace for dinner in quiet, pedestrianised Loutró

world-famous Samariá Gorge (see p. 146) is a little too strenuous, or you have become addicted to gorges, or if you're simply visiting Crete too early or too late in the year, then this easy-to-hike alternative is the solution for you. The Ímbros Gorge is almost as beautiful as its famous sister, but shorter, shallower and not so full of people. It starts in the village of *Ímbros* on the southern edge of the Askífou high plain, and ends about three hours later in Komitádes. The hosts of the tavernas will organise your transfer to the bus stop in *Chóra Sfakíon* (see below) or back to your car in Ímbros for you. *Open during daytime | admission 3 euros | ☐ F4*

17 CHÓRA SFAKÍON
70km / 90 mins from Chaniá by car
Do you love bends? Then you'll travel through paradise when you come here from the northern coast: 20 tight hairpin bends take you from the Askífou high plain down to the Libyan Sea and tiny Chóra Sfakíon, which, despite having a population of only 322, is proud to call itself the capital of the Sfakiá. From here there are ferries along the southern coast to *Paleochóra* (see p. 54) that also stop in *Agía Rouméli*, the destination of any hike through the *Samariá Gorge* (see p. 55 and p.146). Car ferries chug across to *Gávdos*, Europe's southernmost island, where you can spend a night under the starry skies. Or a sea taxi will take you to the completely traffic-free bathing resort of *Loutró* (see p. 57), which also has a tiny beach right on the outskirts. So if you'd like to do a lot of hiking and spend time on the water, this is the perfect place for you for a few days. *☐ E5*

is visited by the spirits of the Cretan freedom fighters who in 1828 tried to occupy the castle but were besieged by the Turks and massacred. You can safely enter on any other day of the year. Right outside is a wide, extremely flat sandy beach. Around 400m further east you can tumble down the sandy slope of 🐾 *Órthi Ámmos Beach* straight into the deep waters. There are only a few buildings along the entire coastal plain, and there is no centre as such, making it ideal for a relaxed, very quiet holiday. 🕮 *F5*

18 LOUTRÓ

70km / 90 mins from Chaniá to Chóra Sfakíon by car, then by boat taxi

Do you yearn for a traffic-free world? Well, your dream can come true in Loutró. The only way to get to this blue-and-white town on the south coast is by boat or on foot; there are no cars. But there are have several tavernas right on the water's edge and no noise at all. You swim from the rocks and in tiny bays. A 30-minute walk will take you to the completely undeveloped shingle beach of *Glikánera*, where fresh and salt water mix. 🕮 *E5*

19 FRANGOKASTÉLLO

80km / 90 mins from Chaniá by car

If you're scared of ghosts, then stay away from this Venetian *castle (April–Oct Wed–Mon 10am–6pm | admission 2 euros)* on 17 May, as that is when it

SLEEP WELL IN CHANIÁ

SO CENTRAL, YET SO CALM

Directly in the heart of Chaniá lies the stylish *Fileas Art Hotel (6 rooms | Odós Pórtou Fragkískou 4–6 | tel. 28 21 00 28 21 | ariahotels.gr/ hotels/fileas-art-hotel | €€)*. It has spacious, good-value double rooms, decorated with local artworks, and is ideal for a stay in town.

HOLIDAY IN AN ECO-VILLAGE

Gentle tourism in the middle of the Cretan mountains! The 🌿 *Milia Mountain Retreat (16 rooms | 3km north of Vlátos | tel. 28 21 04 67 74 | milia.gr | €€)* consists of traditional 16th-century stone houses restored according to ecological principles. It's a peaceful place to unwind in natural surroundings, but there are also plenty of sustainable activities on offer, including guided walks and cookery courses.

RÉTHIMNO

TWO COASTS AND PLENTY IN BETWEEN

Double the fun. In Réthimno and the surrounding area, you will almost always have a view of not one, but two high mountain ranges: the White Mountains and the Ída Mountains. The two biggest island towns, Iráklio and Chaniá, are both only about an hour from Réthimno. And the road between the north and south coasts is extremely well developed, which means you can swim both in the Aegean and in the Libyan Sea in a single day.

Visit a restaurant on Réthimno's harbour at least once to soak up the unique atmosphere

There are pretty villages in the region's mountainous hinterland where you can easily spend half or even a whole day. Réthimno town, the regional capital, has something for everyone – with entertainment lasting well into the night.

A 16km-long sandy beach with lots of water-sports options starts right on the edge of the old town which, with its numerous minarets and mosques, narrow streets and tiny squares, Venetian harbour and castle, is a lovely option worth leaving the beach for.

RÉTHIMNO

You don't necessarily need a hire car in Réthimno. From here, it's easy to reach the south coast by bus and also to go sightseeing in Chaniá or Iráklio.

Thanks to its long town beach, Réthimno is ideal if you want to combine the amenities of a town with a beach holiday.

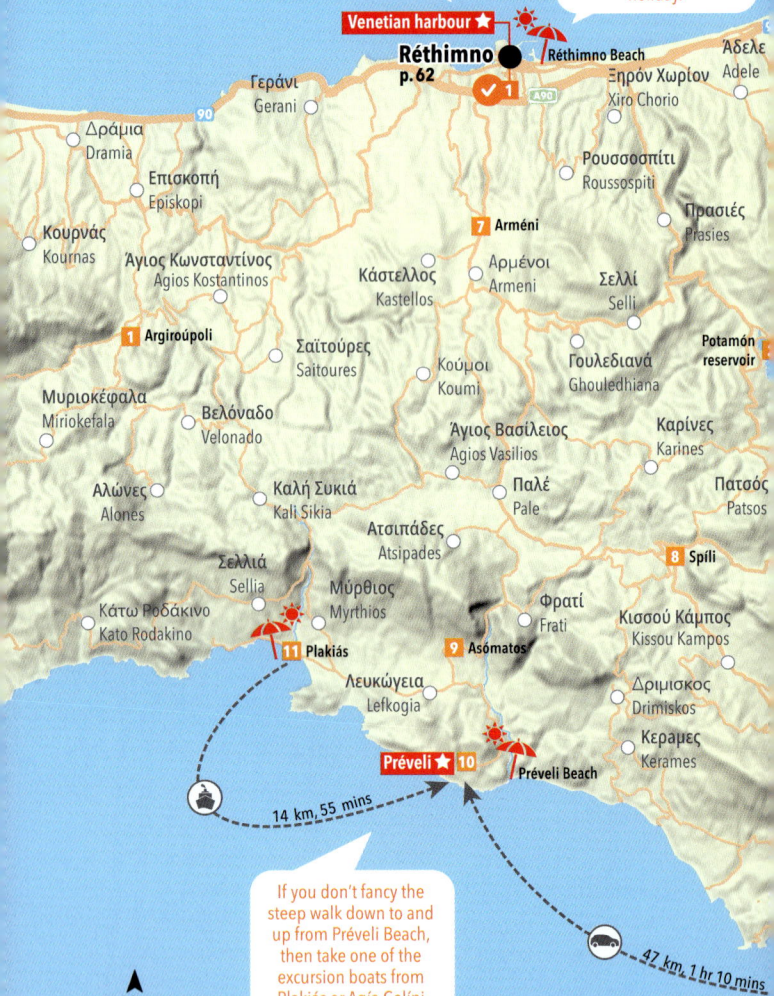

Venetian harbour ★

Réthimno
p. 62

1

Réthimno Beach

Άδελε
Adele

Ξηρόν Χωρίον
Xiro Chorio

Γεράνι
Gerani

Δράμια
Dramia

Ρουσσοσπίτι
Roussospiti

Πρασιές
Prasies

Επισκοπή
Episkopi

7 Arméni

Κούρνας
Kournas

Κάστελλος
Kastellos

Αρμένοι
Armeni

Σελλί
Selli

Άγιος Κωνσταντίνος
Agios Kostantinos

Potamón
reservoir

Σαϊτούρες
Saitoures

Γουλεδιανά
Ghouledhiana

1 Argiroúpoli

Κούμοι
Koumi

Μυριοκέφαλα
Miriokefala

Βελόναδο
Velonado

Άγιος Βασίλειος
Agios Vasilios

Καρίνες
Karines

Αλώνες
Alones

Καλή Συκιά
Kali Sikia

Παλέ
Pale

Πατσός
Patsos

Ατσιπάδες
Atsipades

Σελλιά
Sellia

Μύρθιος
Myrthios

Φρατί
Frati

8 Spíli

Κάτω Ροδάκινο
Kato Rodakino

11 Plakiás

9 Asómatos

Κισσού Κάμπος
Kissou Kampos

Λευκώγεια
Lefkogia

Δριμισκος
Drimiskos

Préveli ★ 10

Préveli Beach

Κεραμες
Kerames

14 km, 55 mins

47 km, 1 hr 10 mins

If you don't fancy the steep walk down to and up from Préveli Beach, then take one of the excursion boats from Plakiás or Agía Galíni instead.

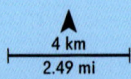

4 km
2.49 mi

L i v i k ó

Kritikó Pélagos

Πάνορμος
Panormos

Σκεπαστή
Skepasti

Μπαλί
Bali

Ρουμελή
Roumeli

Εξάντης
Exandis

Βλυχάδα
Vlichada

90

Πρίνος
Prinos

Melidóni 6

Μελιδόνι
Melidoni

Αγιά
Agia

Πέραμα
Perama

Αλφά
Alfa

Κάμπος Δοξαρού
Kambos Doxaru

Επισκοπή
Episkopi

Γαράζο
Garazo

**Margarites
5**

Άγιος Ιωάννης
Agios Ioannis

Αξός
Axos

4 Eléftherna

Άγιος Μάμας
Agios Mamas

Κάλυβος
Kalyvos

Energetic visitors travel by bike from Réthimno to the Arkádi Monastery; you could also hire a scooter to get here, but please don't copy the locals: wear a helmet!

15km, 25 mins

Χάρκια
Charkia

3 Arkádi Monastery ★

C R E T E

ΚΡΗΤΗ

MARCO POLO HIGHLIGHTS

★ **VENETIAN HARBOUR**
Crete's most beautiful harbour basin, lined with cafés and seafood tavernas ➤ p. 63

★ **ARKÁDI MONASTERY**
This most famous of the island's monasteries is a national shrine ➤ p. 69

★ **PRÉVELI**
Two monasteries, a canyon and a dreamy beach – all very close together ➤ p. 72

Αμάρι
Amari

Μοναστηράκι
Monastiraki

Γερακάρι
Gerakari

Βρύσες
Vrises

Βιζάρι
Vizari

Κουρούτες
Kouroutes

Άνω Μέρος
Ano Meros

Άγιος Ιωάννης
Agios Ioanis

Ορνέ
Orne

MARCO POLO BUCKET LIST

1 ✓ Discover Cretan cuisine

Learn the secrets of Cretan cuisine on a cookery course at *Avlí*, for example ➤ p. 64

Yoga fans can join like-minded enthusiasts around Ágios Pávlos and discover their own personal paradise on Crete.

12 Agía Galíni

Τυμπάκι
Tympaki

Φανερωμένη
Faneromeni

Pélagos

Three lion heads: the Venetian Rimóndi Fountain has been spouting water for 400 years

RÉTHIMNO

(▭ H3) **There are endless shops and tavernas in Réthimno, and lots of pretty little streets take you through residential areas with quaint houses and the typical Turkish timber gazebos. In this town of a mere 39,000 inhabitants you won't have to spend long looking for good cocktail bars and clubs in the evenings; that's taken care of by the town's student scene. Public buses travel to many other towns and beaches in the surrounding area, while cruises along the coast start from the romantic harbour. So boredom is something you will definitely not have to contend with here.**

Réthimno offers a number of cultural activities. The University of Crete has a campus here (as well as in Iráklio and Chaniá) and is home to the Philosophy Faculty – the city has seen itself as the intellectual centre of the island for a long time. Réthimno also has a theatre, a philharmonic society and an adult education college exclusively for women. During the summer there are guest performances by local and foreign music and theatre groups.

SIGHTSEEING

ARCHAEOLOGICAL MUSEUM

So just what is a loo seat doing in a museum? You'll find out when you visit this little archaeological exhibition in an old Venetian church. This particular loo seat is over 1,400 years old, made of stone, and was used for raising boat anchors that had stuck fast. Far more aesthetic are the painted sarcophagi that date back to Minoan times. Try to

WHERE TO START?

Platía Tessáron Mártiron: Buses travelling from Iráklio and Chaniá stop at the Platía Tessáron Mártiron directly at the edge of the old town. South of this *platía* you will find a metered car park which offers the best parking spot – except on Thursdays, which is when the large weekly market is held.

find the naked youth attempting to slay a boar with his sword. *May–Oct Wed–Mon 9am–5pm, Nov–April 8.30am–3.30pm | admission 4 euros | Odós Ethn. Antistáseos |* ⏱ *15 mins*

FORTÉZZA

Time to catch your breath! Only the outer walls are left of the 16th-century Venetian castle. Inside, nature has reclaimed the vast plateau at the tip of the town peninsula. A chapel, a mosque and a few cisterns are the only historic traces that remain. The open-air stage is used for concerts and plays in summer, if there's enough money left in the town's coffers, that is. *May–Oct daily from 8am–7.15pm | admission 5 euros |* ⏱ *1–1½ hrs*

MUSEUM OF CONTEMPORARY CRETAN ART

The island's best art museum not only has works by Cretan artists of the past 50 years, but also provides plenty of space for provocative contemporary exhibitions and performances. *Sat/Sun 10am–3pm, May–Oct Tue–Fri 9am–2pm and 7–9pm, Nov–April Tue–Fri 9am–2pm, Wed, Fri also 6–9pm | admission 3 euros | Odós Messongíou 32 | cca.gr |* ⏱ *20–30 mins*

ODÓS VERNÁRDOU

Looking for a "food boulevard"? In the evening and at night, you need to head for Odós Vernárdou. It has rows of both typical rustic and more contemporary ◗ *rakádika*, serving creative Cretan delights in small portions – just the way the locals like them. Live music is often available in some of the bars. Sometimes you can break with the style and start the evening with classical music: there are occasional concerts in the town's *Odeon*, which is in an old mosque on Odós Vernárdou.

RIMÓNDI FOUNTAIN

The Venetian Rimondi Fountain is busiest during the day. The three stone lions' heads have been spouting water here since 1623. Four streets meet at the fountain, and anyone who is in Réthimno walks past at least once a day. It's the perfect spot to sit in a café and people-watch. *Platía Títu Peticháki*

VENETIAN HARBOUR ⭐

Even if you don't normally frequent fish restaurants, you have to eat at the old Venetian harbour at least once – ideally in the evening, when the buildings on the narrow, semi-circular quay look romantic rather than shabby, and the lighthouse dating back to Turkish times flashes a maritime greeting. Tiny colourful fishing boats are tied up in front of all the tables and chairs outside the fish tavernas, leaving little space for people to walk past.

EATING & DRINKING

AVLÍ

The finest cuisine in all of Réthimno. Cretan and Mediterranean dishes are served here with the slogan "nostalgic with a modern touch". Guests can sit in a courtyard adorned with flowers and under the arches of a Venetian town-house. The cellar is home to over 460 wines.

The six-course tasting menu uses different Cretan olive oils for each dish and, for an additional charge, five different Cretan wines are also served. If you prefer to be in the kitchen yourself, you can also book a ✅ cooking course at Avlí. *Daily from 7pm | Odós*

Xanthoudidou 22 | tel. 28 31 05 82 50 | avli.gr | €€€

KNOSSÓS

"Kráchtes" is what the Cretans call the waiters who talk to all the passers-by, attempting to lure them into their establishment.

INSIDER TIP
Authentic and charming

There is only one place in the Venetian harbour where they don't do this: the Knossós taverna. Here, María runs the service with plenty of charm, while her aunts run the kitchen. The fish is served without frills from the grill, with just oil and lemon as the dressing. *Daily from noon | by the Venetian harbour | €€*

In Odós Arkadíu you will find a huge selection of tablecloths and much more

RÉTHIMNO

Kritikó Pélagos

200 m
219 yd

Museum of Contemporary Cretan Art

Fortézza

Chimaras

Ice Club

Rimóndi Fountain

Astéria

Avlí

Knossós

Venetian harbour ★

Odós Vernárdou

To Rakodikeío

Metropolis

Cul de Sac

Archaeological Museum

B. Psillaki

Ηγουμένου Γαβριήλ
Igoumenou Gavrill

Δημητρακάκη
Dimitrakaki

Θεμιστοκλή
Themistokli

Ελ. Βενιζέλου

Queens Room

Ελ. Βενιζέλου
El. Venizelou

Réthimno Beach

Sofokli
Σοφοκλή

Venizelou
Βενιζέλου

Livingroom

Κουντουριώτη Παύλου
Kountourioti Pavlou

Μοάτσου
Moatsou

Giamboudaki

Εμ. Πορτάλιου
Em. Portaliou

QUEENS ROOM

If you've had enough of Cretan food, come to this stylish club/restaurant to sample Asian snacks, noodles, sashimi, sushi, pancakes, salads and sandwiches. After eating, you can relax with a shisha or head for the dancefloor. *Daily 9am–4am | Odós El. Venizélou 11 | queensroom.gr | €€*

TO RAKODIKEÍO

Of all the *rakádika* that line the old town's "food boulevard", this one offers the greatest choice and the best service, which means it's very popular with the town's students. Don't expect a single dish for yourself; instead, all the dishes are placed in the centre of the table for everyone to share. *Daily 11am–2am | Odós Vernárdou 7 | €–€€*

SHOPPING

The beautiful alley *Odós Arkadíu* in the old town is Réthimno's main shopping street. The locals also buy their shoes and clothes here. Souvenir shops can be found in Antistásseos, Súlion and Paleológou streets and the best Greek delicacies are at *Avlí* at *Armanpatzóglou 40 (Arabatzóglou)*.

SPORT & ACTIVITIES

The 16km sandy beach starts right in the town centre. And it is here where *Ikarus (on the marina pier | tel. 69 95 76 97 10 | watersportikarus.com)* offers all kinds of water sports: jet skiing and water-skiing, parasailing and kite surfing, banana rides and, for the slightly more cautious, even pedalos.

Mountain-biking needs are met by *Kreta Bike (Níkeas 48 | tel. 28 31 07 23 83 | kretabike.com)* on the road to Ádele and Arkádi monastery.

Great fun, especially for families, is to be had with trips on the 👥 *Captain Hook motor boat (adults 25 euros, children from 12.50 euros | departing from the Venetian harbour | dolphin-cruises. com)* with its pirate ship design. The crew comprises buccaneers in full pirate garb, who engage with the children (who can also dress up) and pose for photographs with them. Trips last from one to three hours.

BEACHES

Réthimno Beach is 16km long and begins immediately behind the marina on the edge of the old town. This is where most of the resort hotels of the region are located. Regular bus services are ideal for getting to the beaches of Plakiás and Agía Galíni on the south coast.

WELLNESS

Participants in yoga and meditation courses on the south coast between

In the evening, Odós Vernárdo becomes first a food venue and then a party street

Ágios Pávlos *(🕮 H6)* and Soúda *(🕮 G5)* may sense the earth's magical forces in this beautiful landscape. For details of what's on offer, please visit *yogatravelandbeyond.com* and *yogaholidaysgreece.com*.

FESTIVALS

Réthimno is famous for its Carnival in February/March. On Carnival Sunday the whole town celebrates with a huge procession, accompanied by samba rhythms with Greek lyrics. At the Renaissance Festival *(rfr.gr)* in October, the castle takes centre stage, with a series of concerts and theatre performances taking place across 12 days.

NIGHTLIFE

Where and when do things really get going? Well, before midnight head for ⚑ *rakádika* in the Odós Vernárdou or the fabulously styled cocktail bars between the Venetian harbour and the marina. After midnight, the scene moves to the clubs in the short alleys right behind the Venetian harbour and the part of the Odós Salamínos near the marina.

ASTÉRIA

Open-air cinema and bar underneath the Venetian fortress walls. You'll be able to watch blockbuster movies in their original language. But under the fabulous Cretan starry sky, even the biggest Hollywood celebrities are bound to shrink to the size of starlets. *Admission 8 euros | Odós Melisínu 21/ Odós Smírnis*

CUL DE SAC

The hotspot for warming up, right by the Rimondi Fountain. Also a good place for asking locals where the action will be tonight. *Platía Titu Peticháki 5–9 | culdesac.gr*

ICE CLUB

Students party here at the weekends, dancing to Greek pop and house music. *Odós Salamínos 22 | FB*

LIVINGROOM

The trendy bar on the promenade serves everything the young Greek heart desires, from Greek coffee to French champagne as well as 18 different Greek wines by the glass and tasty ice cream sundaes. In typical Cretan fashion, guests receive a thirst-quenching glass of water before they order. From brunch through to dinner, you can satisfy your hunger here, and then party into the evening. *Odós Eleftheríou Venizélou 5 | living-room.gr*

METROPOLIS

The disco classic with lots of parties and events – from rock concerts to karaoke. Mainstream music is the order of the day. *Odós Neárchou 15, in the Venetian harbour | FB: Metropolis Bar Rethymno*

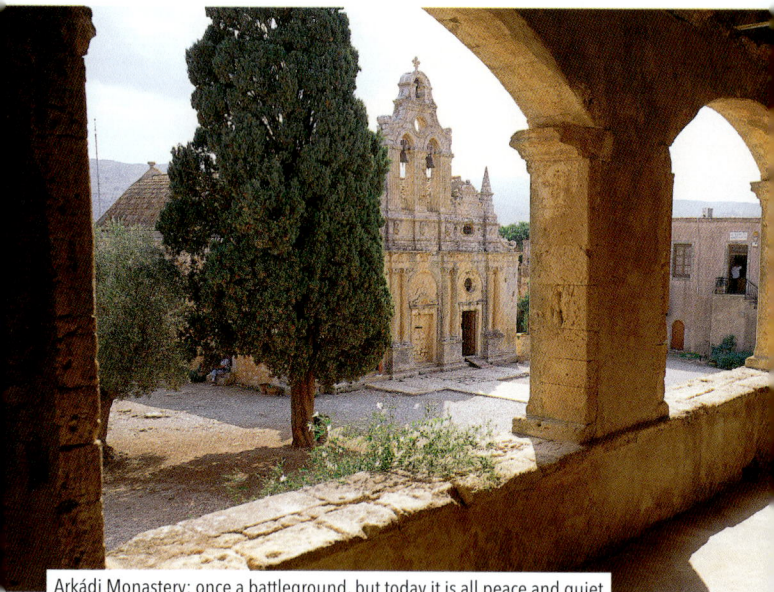

Arkádi Monastery: once a battleground, but today it is all peace and quiet

AROUND RÉTHIMNO

1 ARGIROÚPOLI

25km / 35 mins from Réthimno by car

Mountain villages don't have to be boring – you can easily spend a whole day in this one. Start at the village church with its filigree clock tower. Right next door, a sign draws your attention to some old stone blocks: remains of the antique town of Lappa, which once stood here. Diagonally opposite is the way into the old Venetian village – the entrance arch alone will leave you speechless.

In the village you can buy all kinds of hand creams, gels and lotions made from avocados, which have been grown in the region since the 1990s. You can also get a free map of the town in the shop. The nameless *kafenío* is a nice place to drink a coffee or avocado juice and eat avocado salad. An approximately 30-minute tour of the village takes you to a lovely Roman floor mosaic and the photogenic little chapel of *Agía Paraskeví*. The step down to the churchyard is, in fact, the lid of an antique child-sized sarcophagus. The surrounding unspoilt countryside is sprinkled with ancient graves. Follow the signs on the little road to Káto Póros, 400m further on, and then to the "Holy 5 Virgins". These little *rock graves* are about 2,000 years old.

For lunch, trout and sturgeon, freshly caught in the gushing springs,

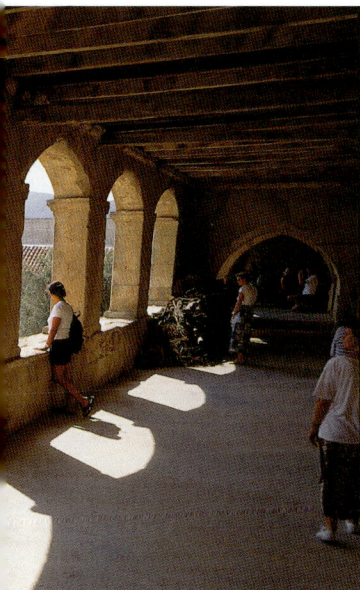

Something wonderful awaits you at *Ágios Antónios Gorge* in the nearby village of Pátsos. A five-minute walk will take you to a gorge where the *tiny cave chapel of St Antónios* offers fascinating examples of the Orthodox belief in miracles: notes with prayers have been slipped into cracks in the rocks; romper suits hang inside the church, and crutches have been placed in the corners. About 350m before the entrance to the gorge, it is worth stopping at the family-run *Kourkouloú winery (Mon–Fri 10.30am–5.30pm | kourkoulouwinery.gr)*, which is not just for wine lovers, although it does offer wine tastings, including an informative tour (book online in advance). *H4*

await you in the tavernas. To dine in a historic ambience, head for *Paliós Mylos (daily from 11am | €€)*, set in and around an old water mill. On the way back to Réthimno, you can stop at the modern shop, which makes innovative use of another natural product: carob. At the *Creta Carob Shop (cretacarob.com)*, you will find all sorts of natural products made with carob, from syrup to tea, coffee and cocoa. *G4*

2 POTAMÓN RESERVOIR

22km / 35 mins from Réthimno by car

Crete's newest and largest reservoir is a nice destination for those seeking the great outdoors. The view of the lake and the mountains that frame it is best enjoyed from the *Café Gidóspita (€)* near the 310m-long dam wall.

3 ARKÁDI MONASTERY ★

20km / 40 mins from Réthimno by car

Can mass suicide be a heroic deed? Crete's clear answer to that is "yes". Which is why the monastery on an isolated high plain has been declared a national shrine of the island. In 1866, Cretan insurgents were entrenched here, together with their wives and children, against approaching Turkish troops. When, after a two-day siege, the Turks broke into the monastery, the insurgents all gathered in the powder magazine and blew themselves up rather than face rape and enslavement. Over 900 Christians died. The story of this "heroic" suicide quickly spread throughout the world, and ultimately led to Crete being annexed to the Greek motherland in 1913. The bones and skulls of numerous victims are now on display in glass cabinets in the *Mausoleum* opposite the entrance to the monastery. Flowers are still placed on an altar in the now-roofless powder magazine, while the story of Arkádis is told in more detail in the *Monastery Museum (May, Sept, Oct daily 9am–7pm, June–Aug daily 9am–8pm, otherwise daily 9am–5pm | admission 4 euros).* ⟁ *J4*

4 ELÉFTHERNA
22km / 30 mins from Réthimno by car

Since the Minoans were immigrants from Asia rather than being Greek, the excavations at Eléftherna are extremely important to today's Cretans. Genuine Hellenes lived here 2,000 years ago, something that is also emphasised in the state-of-the-art *museum (Wed–Mon April–Oct 10am–6pm, Nov–March 8.30am–3.30pm | admission 6 euros).* It is also confirmed by the *three archaeological sites* that you can explore on a half-day hike from here – but be sure to check at the museum that they are still open to the public. For an excellent map of the entire ancient town, visit short.travel/kre9. And you will need it! By the way, you can explore antique cisterns in the neighbouring village of Archéa Eléftherna, which is quite good fun. ⟁ *J4*

> **INSIDER TIP**
> **Mapping the past**

5 MARGARÍTES
27km / 35 mins from Réthimno by car

If you are still looking for souvenirs, you'll find an excellent selection in Margarítes. More than 🍃 20 ceramicists work here in studios along the village street, producing objects of art and kitsch, useful items or simply pretty things. In the midst of them all, every morning, landlady Eléni prepares her legendary moussaká at *Gianousákis (daily from 10am | €).* ⟁ *J4*

6 MELIDÓNI
31km / 45 mins from Réthimno by car

Now you have to be brave. That's because the biggest attraction in this pretty, old village is *Reptisland (summer daily 9am–6pm, April/May and Oct Mon–Sat 9am–5pm | admission 5 euros | next to the petrol station at the north entrance to the village),* with scorpions, tarantulas, lizards and giant snakes from all over the world. The Papakostánti brothers, whose animals they are, have fulfilled their exotic animal childhood dream here.

If you would then like to relax, you can drive up to the *Melidóni stalactite cave (summer daily 9am–6pm, winter Sat/Sun 10am–4pm | admission 4 euros),* which is only 2km away. The bones and skulls on the altar that commemorate a Turkish massacre in 1824 will hardly alarm you now. On the side of the road into the neighbouring village of Agía you'll see charcoal burners, who still produce charcoal the traditional way in piles under the open sky.

If you would like to take something with you to remind you of this special place, go to the modern 🐟 *Paráskakis olive oil factory (open daily | admission free)* on the road to Pérama. Home

INSIDER TIP
With open arms

owner Ioánna and her mother are very friendly and only too happy to answer any questions you may have about Crete. Those who buy their olive oil here will carry these memories forever. Opposite, in the *Apíthano Honey Museum (Mon–Sat 10am–6pm | admission free)* you can learn all about Cretan honey and try different types. On the village square, Katerini welcomes you in the *Carob & Olive (€)*, a taverna where the speciality is carob biscuits and yogurt with olives and beetroot marinated in honey. *K3*

7 ARMÉNI

11km / 15 mins from Réthimno by car

Crete's prettiest cemetery is situated in a forest of kermes and vallonea oaks. Over the past 50 years, archaeologists have excavated more than 230 tombs. The deceased were buried there about 3,300 years ago. The tombs are all of different sizes, and you can enter many of them. It's not at all spooky; in fact, it's actually a great setting for a picnic in the countryside. *April–Oct Mon 9am–5pm, Nov–March Mon 8.30am–3.30pm | admission 3 euros | H4*

8 SPÍLI

30km / 45 mins from Réthimno by car

On the drive between the north and south coasts, stop at the large, old mountain village of Spíli. Have coffee on the shady *platía* with water bubbling forcefully from the numerous lions' heads of its Venetian fountain, and then drive on. *H5*

The cisterns of Archéa Eléftherna were carved out of the rock 2,300 years ago

You can visit Préveli Beach on a boat trip

9 ASÓMATOS

30km / 40 mins from Réthimno by car

The village priest Michális Georgioulákis (1921–2008) always did everything differently, consequently his village museum *Oriseum (daily 10am–3pm | admission 4 euros)* is unique. On display is everything that he collected from surrounding villages, bought at flea markets or inherited over 60 years.

Afterwards, you can buy pretty ceramics in the *Hydria studio (ceramic. gr)* on the main road – everything is still made in the traditional way on a potter's wheel. Visitors are allowed to have a go too. *H5*

10 PRÉVELI ★

37km / 1 hr from Réthimno by car

You can spend an entire day of your holiday at Préveli. There is the terrific *Préveli Beach*, a lovely taverna, an old bridge, two monasteries and a canyon full of palm trees – short walk included. Coming from the main road, after 2km you first cross a photogenic bridge with a lovely arch that farmers used to cross with their donkeys. By the rushing mountain stream below is a good *taverna (daily from 10am | €)* with ducks outside that you can feed. A further 600m on, below the road, are the accessible ruins of the *Káto Préveli Monastery (admission 2.50 euros)*. The road ends 3.2km further on at the *Piso Préveli Monastery (Mon–Sat 9am–1.30pm and 3.30–7pm, Sun 9am–7pm | admission 3 euros)*. In 1941, the monks hid British soldiers here until they could be picked up by submarines.

Between Káto and Píso Préveli, a cul-de-sac branches off towards the coast, and ends at a car park *(2 euros/day)*. A steep footpath takes you from there down to the Préveli stream in about 30 minutes. A river with cold water flows across the beach (about 200m long) into the sea from the Kourtaliátiko Gorge, a narrow canyon overgrown by palm trees. *H5*

11 PLAKIÁS

40km / 1 hr from Réthimno by car

The *sandy beach* at Plakiás is over 800m long, and widens to the west into a dune landscape – where you can also obtain an all-over tan if you so want. Almost all of the bars and tavernas are right beside the water, and there are daily boat trips out from the tiny harbour to *Préveli Beach*. Signposted, fairly steep hiking trails lead through olive groves, up into the mountain villages of *Mýrthios* and *Selliá*, where you will find craft shops as well as good tavernas. There is affordable jewellery in Mýrthios from Josíf Petrákis at *Líthos Nature Collection*, and in Selliá from Jánnis and Angelika at *Ikaros*. Jánnis Méxis and Pinélopi Kostogiánni shape fabulous items out of wood and modelling clay at Art & Nature in Selliá. The *Anso* travel agency organises guided tours and mountain-bike rides. *G5*

12 AGÍA GALÍNI

55km / 75 mins from Réthimno by car

If you are anything but shy, then you'll feel completely at home in this village, which has the pretty name of "Holy Tranquillity". The densely built centre stretches from the harbour up a narrow valley that has most of the hotels and guesthouses on its slopes. The actual centre is formed by three vertical and two horizontal streets full of shops, bars and cafés. Most of the tavernas reach up several floors right next to the harbour square, their roof gardens and terraces sparkling with lights in the evenings between the sky and the sea. All village life happens in an area measuring about 100m x 200m, so you'll keep meeting the same people.

A good place for a rendezvous is the modern memorial to the mythical aviators Daedalus and Icarus on the terrace above the harbour. There's swimming off a long, narrow beach 200m to the north of the harbour. And throughout the day several boats head out to the beaches in the area and as far as *Préveli Beach* (see p. 72).

Delicious Cretan food is served at taverna *Onar,* at the harbour. *J6*

SLEEP WELL IN RÉTHIMNO

ELEGANT OASIS

The *Rimondi Boutique hotel (33 rooms | Odós Xanthoudídou 10 | tel. 28 31 05 10 01 | hotelsrimondi.hotelbrain.com | €€–€€€)* consists of two Venetian buildings in the alleyways of the old town. If you're looking for romantic and elegant accommodation, then this place's tasteful rooms and suites will appeal to you. The charming inner courtyards feature small pools that create a stylish, relaxing atmosphere.

SWEEPING VIEWS

The well-kept *Mirthea Suites (4 suites | tel. 69 76 88 06 66 | mirtheasuites.gr | €€–€€€)* in Mírthios enjoy breathtaking views of Plakiás Bay, but if a five-minute walk to the sea seems too much, then there's also a communal pool on site. The décor combines natural materials with modern features; one of the suites even has its own whirlpool.

IRÁKLIO

THE HEARTBEAT OF THE ISLAND

Landed safely? Every year, more than six million passengers land at Iráklio (Heraklion) airport, and more than one-third of all Cretans live in the city's greater metropolitan area. From a distance, Iráklio (city pop. almost 180,000) may look like an urban sprawl, but fear not! The city centre is pretty, clearly laid out and, above all, bursting with urban life. By day and night.

Large hotels are centred on the northern coast between Heraklion and Mália, but even these resorts don't compare to the kind of mass

Having a chat: everyone meets up at the Morosíni Fountain

tourism that is found on the coasts of other countries. And, on the southern coast, independent travellers will feel completely at home. Between the two coasts are vineyards, the fertile Messará Plain and two wild mountain ranges. Excursions take you back 3,500 years to the Minoan palace towns of Festós and Knossós, the centres of Europe's first advanced civilisation. The remains of five-storey houses can still be seen, and the unique artefacts discovered at these sites are on display in the Archaeological Museum in Iráklio.

IRÁKLIO

Kritikó   Pélagos

Nisí Día

Σκεπαστή
Skepasti

Μπαλί
Bali

Σίσσες
Sisses

Αχλάδα
Achlada

Πέραμα
Perama

Fódele **9**

Archaeological Museum ★

After your day trip to Tílissos, Anógia and Zonianá, travel back to Iráklio via a slightly longer route along the coastal highway and finish your day with a dip in the sea, at Agía Pelagía, for example.

Ammoudará Beach

Γάζι
Gazi

Iráklio
p. 78

✓ **3**

6 Tílissos

Knossós ★ **1**

Zonianá **8**
5 ✓

7 Anógia

Καμάρι
Kamari

Σταυράκια
Stavrakia

Σκαλάνι
Skalani

C R E T E
ΚΡΗΤΗ

Άγιος Μύρωνας
Agios Mironas

97

Archánes
2
✓ **1**

Φουρφουράς
Fourfouras

Κάτω Ασίτες
Kato Asites

Κουρούτες
Kouroutes

The wineries in Crete's largest wine region are all signposted. Just pull up where you fancy. Don't forget to spit out the wine during a tasting; you are driving, after all!

68 km, 1 hr 20 mins

60 km, 1 hr 10 mins

Zarós **15**

If the beach at Mátala is too crowded for you, follow the locals to Kommós Beach. Here, you're sure to find a peaceful stretch of sand.

Μακρές
Makres

97

Στόλοι
Stoli

100 km, 1 hr 45

12 Vóri

Górtis **14**

Άγιοι Δέκα
Agii Deka

11 **Festós** ★ **13** Míres

Πρετόρια
Protoria

Kommós
Beach

10 Pitsídia

Πετροκεφάλι
Petrokefali

Πλάτανος
Platanos

Στέρνες
Sternes

Πύργος
Pyrgos

Red
Beach

Mátala ★
p. 89

Πηγαιδάκια
Pigaidakia

Άγιος Κύριλλος
Agios Kyrillos

Παράνυμφοι
Paranimfi

Λέντας
Lentas

Livikó
Pélagos

▲

10 km
6.21 mi

★ **ARCHAEOLOGICAL MUSEUM**
Treasures of the Minoan civilisation
➤ p. 78

★ **KNOSSÓS**
Captivating ruins of archaeology's
"Disneyland" ➤ p. 83

★ **MÁTALA**
Hippie caves, old fishing village, sandy
beaches – it's easy to get lost in your
memories ➤ p. 89

★ **FESTÓS**
A Minoan palace with a fantastic view
➤ p. 91

Use the bus to travel between your hotel in
Mália or Chersónisos and Iráklio. It's more environmentally friendly than using a car and will save your
nerves when it comes to finding a parking space.

Amnissós Beach

Ανάληψη
Analipsi

Σίσι
Sisi

Μίλατος
Milátos

3 Goúrnes

Chersónisos 4

Μάλια Beach

Νεάπολη
Neapoli

Ελούντα
Flounta

Χερσόνισος
Hersonissos

A90

✓ **4 5** Mália

Επισκοπή
Episkopi

Ποταμιές
Potamies

Μοχός
Mochos

90

Καστέλι
Kasteli

Κασταμόνιτσα
Kastamonitsa

Τζερμιάδο
Tzermiado

Άγιος Νικόλαος
Agios Nikolaos

Αρκαλοχώρι
Arkalohori

Γεράκι
Geraki

Άγιος Γεώργιος
Agios Georgios

You can get to the
Lassíthi Plateau (see
p.105) from Ágios
Nikólaos but also, in
under an hour, from
Chersónisos and Mália.

Καλό Χωριό
Kalo Chorio

Έμπαρος
Embaros

Μάλες
Males

Καλαμαύκα
Kalamafka

Γαρίπα
Garipa

Σκινιάς
Skinias

Μάρθα
Martha

Άνω Βιάννος
Ano Viannos

1 ✓ Discover Cretan cuisine

Learn the secrets of Cretan cuisine on a
cookery course at *Bakáliko*, for example.
➤ p.84

3 ✓ Feel the earth move

Try out Iráklio's *Earthquake Simulator* for
an experience that you wouldn't want to
have in real life! ➤ p.79

4 ✓ Dance till you drop

Incredibly, *Mália* has 60 *nightclubs*, so you
can choose a different place to party every
night. ➤ p.86

5 ✓ Descend into the underworld

The *Sventóni cave* is a wonderland of
stalactites, created by water droplets over
millennia. ➤ p.88

IRÁKLIO

(*M–N4*) **Road traffic has been brought well under control in recent years; traffic lights have been removed and many pedestrian precincts created, which means there is now even more room for tavernas and street cafés. Iráklio has the best shopping on the island; its museums are among the most important in Greece, and there is much to discover from Venetian times.**

WHERE TO START?

Venetian harbour: In order to avoid the problem of finding parking in Iráklio, it is best to go there by bus. If you arrive by car, you can park along the shore at the commercial port (partly free), then walk in a westerly direction for about five to 15 minutes to the Venetian harbour on the edge of the old town.

SIGHTSEEING

ÁGIOS MÁRKOS CATHEDRAL

The oldest Venetian church built in 1239 (close to the *Morosíni Fountain*) today hosts concerts and exhibitions. The monolithic pillars of the basilica date back to ancient times. *Opening times vary | admission free | Platía Liontaríon |* ⏱ *15 mins*

ÁGIOS MINÁS CATHEDRAL

Do you like looking through colourful picture books? The cathedral of Iráklio, about 150 years old, is just that – a picture book that up to 8,000 people can read at the same time. Cupolas, arches and walls are completely covered in paintings of numerous biblical stories. Turn it into a game, and try to find the story of the birth of Jesus and his crucifixion. Any others that you find will certainly earn you additional points in heaven! *Usually open during the day | admission free | Odós Agíou Miná 25 |* ⏱ *15 mins*

INSIDER TIP
A different kind of quiz

ÁGIOS TÍTOS CHURCH

Holy hoo-ha? Many Cretans would beg to differ. They believe that the skull in the silver reliquary in the side chapel on the left really is that of St Titus, the island's first bishop from almost 2,000 years ago. *Daily 7am–8pm | admission free | Platía Agíou Títou |* ⏱ *5–10 mins*

ARCHAEOLOGICAL MUSEUM ⭐

If not here, then where? The two-storey museum contains more finds from Minoan times than all of the other museums in the world combined. And as well as noble art, it contains numerous items that speak to us of everyday life here – about 3,500 years ago. On display are Minoan house façades made from tiles, a board game, clay model ships and houses, jewellery and a number of seals. One of the most valuable pieces is a vessel in the shape of a

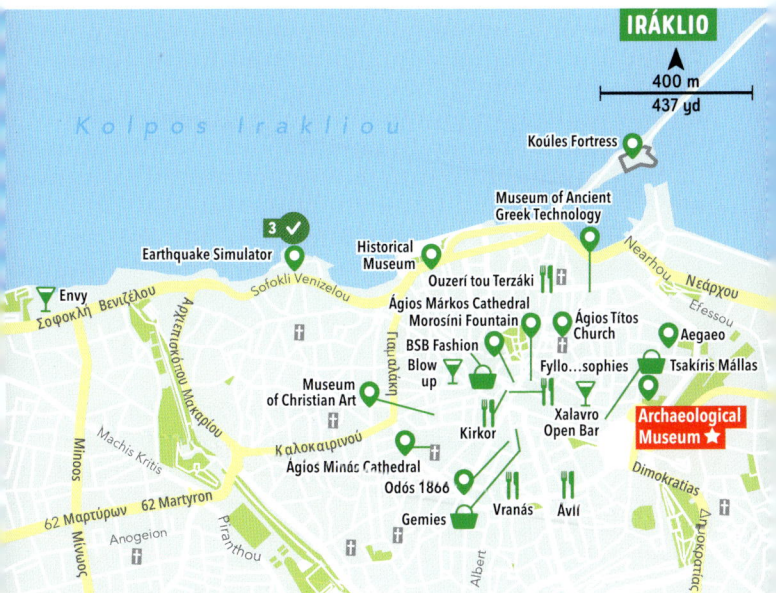

Map labels:
IRÁKLIO
400 m
437 yd
Kolpos Irakliou
Koúles Fortress
Museum of Ancient Greek Technology
Historical Museum
Earthquake Simulator
Sofokli Venizélou
Ouzerí tou Terzáki
Envy
Σοφοκλή Βενιζέλου
Αρχιεπισκόπου Μακαρίου
Άgios Márkos Cathedral
Morosíni Fountain
BSB Fashion
Blow up
Άgios Títos Church
Aegaeo
Fyllo…sophies
Tsakíris Mállas
Παπαλάκη
Archaeological Museum
Museum of Christian Art
Kirkor
Xalavro Open Bar
Καλοκαιρινού
Machis Kritis
Minoos
Άgios Minás Cathedral
Odós 1866
Gemies
Vranás
Avlí
Dimokratias
Δημοκρατίας
62 Μαρτύρων 62 Martyron
Μίνωος
Anogeion
Piranthou
Albert
Nearhou
Νεάρχου
Efessou
Eressou

---

bull's head carved from soapstone, with rock crystal eyes and a mother of pearl mouth; another is a rhyton, a drinking and alms vessel made of shimmering rock crystal. The 3,500-year-old Phaistos disc is particularly fascinating. It is covered on both sides with a spiral of 241 hieroglyphics stamped into the clay, the meaning of which has never been conclusively explained. The murals from the Palace of Knossós and the Minoan villas are staggeringly beautiful – they look like prehistoric photo wallpaper. *April–Oct Tue 10am–8pm, Wed–Mon 8am–8pm; Nov–March Tue 10am–5pm, Wed–Mon 8.30am–3.30pm | admission 12 euros, tickets online at heraklion museum.gr | Platía Eleftherías/Odós Xanthudínu | ⏱ 1½–2 hrs*

EARTHQUAKE SIMULATOR ✓

What does it feel like when the earth quakes? That is something that no one would really want to experience, but in the simulator of the *Museum of Natural History* it's both interesting and perfectly safe. In a replica of an old classroom, earthquakes of various forces give you a good shaking every half-hour. *Mon–Fri 9am–5pm, Sat/Sun 10am–6pm | admission 8 euros | Leof. Sof. Venizélou | nhmc.uoc.gr*

HISTORICAL MUSEUM

What did Iráklio look like 400 years ago? A large wooden model shows it clearly at a scale of 1:500. Also interesting are the medieval hand grenades made of glass and ceramic; Cretan folk costumes and art; an office of the *Sorbás* author Níkos Kazantzákis;

and for art lovers, two small paintings by El Greco. *April–Oct daily 9am–5pm, Nov–March Mon–Fri 9am–3.30 pm, Sat 10am–4pm | admission 8 euros | Odós Lysimachou Kalokerinou 7 | historical-museum.gr | ⏱ 20–30 mins*

KOÚLES FORTRESS

This will get your blood flowing. First you climb under the dark arches of the Venetian harbour fort and up onto the roof to look out over the old town to the Cretan mountains. Then you can join the joggers running a circuit along the approx. 1km pier. *April–Oct Wed–Mon 8am–6pm, Nov–March Wed–Mon 8.30am–3.30pm | admission 4 euros | at the pier of the fishing harbour | ⏱ 15–25 mins*

MOROSÍNI FOUNTAIN

Arranging somewhere to meet? The Venetian "lion" fountain is the general meeting place of the city. It's where all the main day- and night-time streets come together: the wide pedestrian street is 25 Avgústou, the main shopping streets are Dédalu, 1866 and Kalokerinú, and the nightlife areas are Chandakós, Milátou and Kagiampí. The fountain square itself is perfect for a *gyros* in the hand or a *bugátsa* in a café, with people from all over the world as a source of constant entertainment. *Platía Venizélou*

MUSEUM OF ANCIENT GREEK TECHNOLOGY 👥

Did you know that the Ancient Greeks had such things as cinemas and computers? No? Then you should make a point of visiting this museum, which displays Ancient Greek objects in a Venetian palace. With over 60 replicas of everything from steam engines to navigation tools to robots, the interactive and video displays bring the technology of the ancient world to life. Interesting for kids, too. *May–Oct daily 10am–6pm, Nov–April Mon–Fri 9am–3pm, Sat/Sun 10am–5pm | admission 7 euros, children (6–17 years) 3.50 euros | Odós Epimenídou 18 | short. travel/kre10 | ⏱ 45–60 mins*

MUSEUM OF CHRISTIAN ART

Icons are not for everyone, but for those who do appreciate them, here are six masterpieces by Michaíl Damaskinós, the most important representative of the Cretan style of holy art in the 16th century. *April–Oct Mon–Sat 9.30am–6pm | admission 4 euros | Platía Ekaterínis | ⏱ 15–25 mins*

ODÓS 1866

Although the 200m-long street is no longer a traditional market for locals, there's still plenty going on. It's an excellent place to shop for culinary souvenirs, to pop into rather old-fashioned *kafenía* or modern bistros. The best place to sit is at the eastern end of the street beside the Venetian Bembo Fountain, which is adorned by a headless statue.

EATING & DRINKING

AVLÍ

Hidden away in a welcoming inner courtyard, Avlí is a family concern: Tássos, the father, and Mariléna, the daughter, are in charge of service,

Browse in the shade on Odós 1866, where market traders have everything on display

while Katerína, the mother, prepares typical Greek delicacies in the open kitchen – from tasty starters to all kinds of barbecue dishes. Mariléna translates and explains everything on the menu to diners and is also a competent sommelier who can recommend suitable wine pairings to go with the food. *Mon–Sat from 2pm | Smírnis 31 | tel. 28 13 01 77 84 | €–€€*

KIRKOR & FYLLO...SOPHIES

Fancy something sweet? These two cafés serve *bougátsa*, a type of semolina pudding with filo pastry, dusted with lots of icing sugar. Make sure to eat it over a napkin, otherwise you will look as if it has snowed! A savoury version is the *bougátsa tirí* made with a sheep's cheese filling. *Daily from 6am | Morosini Fountain | €*

OUZERI TOU TERZÁKI

Because Cretans like to spend a long time discussing what to eat with everyone else at the table, an old custom is coming back into fashion: the waiter presents the guests with a list instead of a menu, and they then put a tick against all the things they'd like to eat. There are plenty of unusual dishes as well as all the usuals – why not try Cretan snails? *Daily from noon | Odós Marinélli 17 | tel. 28 10 22 14 44 | ouzeri-terzakis.gr | €€*

VRANÁS

Fish doesn't come any fresher than in this small taverna on the edge of the fish market in Iráklio. Watch what happens when you order fish for lunch: the landlord shouts your order to the fishmonger

INSIDER TIP
Straight from net to pan

Sofokli Venizélou waterfront

across the lane who promptly delivers it to the kitchen. *Mon–Sat 11am to midnight | Odós Karteroú 13 | tel. 28 10 28 85 54 | €*

SHOPPING

BSB FASHION
BSB, one of the biggest fashion companies in Greece, is currently expanding worldwide and on the web. From denim to formal, metallic to partywear – there's plenty of choice, and it's different from what you normally find at home! *Odós Idís 26–28 | bsbfashion.com*

GEMIES
Chrístos sells handcrafted silver, copper, brass and leather jewellery in his shop on Iráklio's market street. Most of the pieces are one-offs and feature semi-precious stones of every shape and colour, from minimalist designs to more boho styles that will appeal to all ages. *Odós 1866 39 | @gemies.gr*

TSAKÍRIS MÁLLAS
Art for the feet: the women of Crete love going out in the most progressive shoes, sandals and boots made by Greek shoe artists – but there's also plenty on offer for the more conservative, as well as for men and children, all usually at reasonable prices. *Odós Dédalou 30–32 | tsakirismallas.gr*

SPORT & ACTIVITIES

The most common types of water sport are available on the city beaches of Iráklio. If you like being on the water and if for you the journey is the destination, then try a six-hour sailing trip from *Set Sails Crete (80 euros | setsailscrete.com)*, which will take you from the Venetian harbour to the uninhabited island of Día. While your physical wellbeing is taken care of on the boat, you can relax, swim or snorkel. Romantics choose the afternoon tour and return at sunset. Those who prefer something more luxurious can also head to the island of Día on the catamaran from *Cavo Yachts (120 euros | cavoyachts.gr)*.

BEACHES

Are you getting too hot in the city? *Municipal buses (astiko-irakleiou.gr)* take you to the nearby beaches for a very small fee: Line 6 leaves from the bus terminal by the harbour and runs to long sandy beaches at *Ammoudára*, while Line 7 (also leaves from the bus terminal) runs to the beach of Karterós and the sandy beach of *Amnissós*, both located east of the airport.

WELLNESS

AEGAEO

The spa at Hotel Aquila Atlantis offers a 20-minute body-care treatment using Cretan herbs that will set you up for the rest of the day. Other services include aloe treatments, face yoga and massages. *Hotel Aquila Atlantis | Odós Igías 2 | tel. 21 07 00 50 00 | hotels.aegeospas.gr/atlantis-hotel*

NIGHTLIFE

In the evenings young Iráklion people meet in the bars and music cafés at ⚑ *Odós Milatou,* as well as in the *mezedopolía* along the Kagiampí. A more alternative crowd frequents the little bars in the *Odós Chandakós.* Dance clubs open around midnight at the western edge of the old town on the coastal road *Sofokli Venizélou.*

BLOW UP

More of a pub with music than a bar, and more alternative than mainstream. Lots of students. DJs every evening, sometimes live soul, blues and funk. *Daily from 8pm | 15 Odós Psaromilíngon*

ENVY

Clubbing like you do at home? That would be the Envy Club, a firm fixture in the city's young nightlife scene. There's often live Greek pop music in summer, when you'll have to pay for admission *(20 euros including 1 drink).* During the day you can also enjoy your coffee here with a view of the sea! *Daily from 9am | Sofokli Venizélou, opposite Tálos Centre*

XALAVRO OPEN BAR

In the summer, the town's youth flock to this trendy open-air bar between the old walls for its great atmosphere and creative cocktails. The sister restaurant, opposite, serves fusion food. *Daily from 10am | Milátou 10 | xalavro. gr*

AROUND IRÁKLIO

1 KNOSSÓS ★

5km / 10 mins from Iráklio by bus

The no. 1 of the island's top sights. Over 3,500 years ago, the so-called Palace of Knossós was already a major town with a population of perhaps 80,000. While the rest of us were still living in caves, some people in Knossós were living in four-storey houses with sewage systems, paved roads and squares. Pretty frescoes adorned the walls, and works of art of a unique elegance were created in workshops, while the people stored provisions in vast jugs in storage rooms. And although the people of Knossós used a form of writing, they did so mainly for recording the dates of their stores and provisions; they passed nothing of themselves and their history on to us.

The Englishman Sir Arthur Evans unearthed the settlement in the first quarter of the 20th century – and then rebuilt part of it, which is why, unlike in other places, you can see more than just a few layouts and walls. Columns and pillars support many a roof, and murals adorn the walls. You will be able to imagine life in those ancient times. Also of help are the postcards with the coloured reconstruction drawing of the whole complex, which you can buy near the cash desk.

The "palace" was without doubt a multipurpose building. Religious ceremonies played a large part. In festivals, processions progressed through long corridors, as can be seen in the frescoes on the wall of the west corridor at the beginning of a tour. They were heading for the large central courtyard. Adjoining it to the west are a number of dark halls, such as the pillar crypts, which imitate cave sanctuaries. Sir Arthur even found a kind of throne in one room. Perhaps it was left unoccupied for a deity, or perhaps it was used by a priestess. He believed it might have been reserved for the legendary king. He also believed he had found, in the former four-storey building on the eastern side of the central courtyard, the rooms of the king and queen, both of which had a water closet, although there is some doubt about this today. It is more likely to

have been a building with luxury apartments. *April–Oct daily 8am–8pm, Nov–March 8.30am–5pm | admission 15 euros, online tickets available at hhticket.gr | from Iráklio the city bus no. 2 leaves from the bus station at the harbour and from the bus stop in front of house no. 62 in Odos 1821, every 20 mins to Knossós.* ▢ N4

2 ARCHÁNES ✦

15km / 20 mins from Iráklio by car
Despite their proximity to the island's capital, the villages around Iráklio have preserved their rural character. Archánes is a large wine village that attracts locals at weekends. The come to eat at the tavernas around its appealing central *platía*, such as *Bakáliko (closed Wed | tel. 28 10 75 11 17 | bakalikocrete.com | €€).*

INSIDER TIP
Cretan flavours

It serves new interpretations of Cretan cuisine and also offers ✔ cookery courses and wine tastings.

Continue your wine tour in the surrounding region with its 30,000ha of vines. The growers here cultivate international grape varieties but also local ones, such as Liátiko, Vilána, Kotsifáli and Mandilári, which can be tasted in the wineries themselves between April and October. Try, for example, *Lyrarákis (daily 10.30am–7pm | tasting from €18 | lyrarakis.com)* in Alágni. ▢ N5

3 GOÚRNES

10km / 20 mins from Iráklio by car
Goúrnes is an unspectacular coastal resort, but it is also a fun family destination, thanks to the abandoned US

air force base which has been redeveloped with some exciting attractions (a luxury hotel complex with casino and shopping mall is due to be added in the future). The highlight is the 👹 *Cretaquarium (April–Oct daily 9.30am–7pm, Nov–March 9.30am–4pm | admission 12 euros, children 5–17 years 6 euros, under 5s free | cretaquarium.gr)*, where over 2,000 sea creatures, from plankton to sharks, will teach you about the Mediterranean's marine world.

Just round the corner, in the 👹 *Dinosauria Park (May-Oct daily 10am–6pm | admission from 12 euros, children 3–12 years from 10 euros | dinosauriapark.com)*, you can get up close and personal with 50 species of dinosaur, some of which are animatronic. There are also virtual reality and "5-D" exhibits, and even a dino-hospital with a maternity suite! If the kids get peckish, visit *Taverna Krítes (€–€€)*, which is also located here and has a children's playground.

4 CHERSÓNISOS

26km / 25 mins from Iráklio by car

This is where it's at! *Liménas Chersónisou* is the international party metropolis on the island. The traffic-free beach promenade is almost 2km long with lots of tavernas, café bars, pubs and music clubs. About 200m from the beach is the equally long main street with hundreds of shops and more pubs and restaurants.

If you are keen to learn about Minoan culture, start with the Palace of Knossós

It's never boring here, which is why people are also happy to accept that in the town itself, there is too little beach for too many people. Instead, they use the many hotel pools or the 🐟 *Star Beach Water Park (admission free)* on the northern outskirts of the town with its water slides and party sounds that start in the morning.

When you want to escape from the noise and bustle, head to the mountainside villages of *Koutouloufári* and *Piskopianó*, which are about 20 minutes away. With their narrow streets and natural brick buildings, they are every bit as idyllic as you probably expected Crete to be. You can easily spend an evening in the elegant cocktail bars. If you prefer tavernas on a *platía*, visit the nearby village of Chersónisos. (Until 50 years ago, Liménas Chersónisou was merely a poor boat mooring for the village.) If you want to learn about life on Crete before the tourists came, visit the private open-air museum *Lychnostátis (Sun–Fri 9am–2pm | admission 8 euros | lychnostatis.gr)* on the eastern outskirts of the town. Its exhibits are informative and entertaining.

🐵 *Labyrinth Park (mid-April–Oct, Tue–Fri 10am–6pm, Sat/Sun 10am–8pm | admission 12 euros, children 4–11 years 8 euros | labyrinthpark.gr)*, just 3km southwest of Chersónisos, is an adventure village offering labyrinths, a mini-farm and more. There is plenty of fun for families who are prepared to pay extra for additional activities such as archery, horse riding or pottery. 📖 *O4*

5 MÁLIA

37km / 35 mins from Iráklio by car

This expansive holiday resort is usually firmly in the hands of young British visitors. ✅ Nowhere else are the screens in the sports bars bigger, the quad bikes more numerous on the streets, and the tattoo studios open later at night. Shots and beer flow freely – and yet potatoes still thrive in the deep-red fields among all the bars, clubs and hotels.

The fine 🏖 sandy beach is lovely and wide, and miles long. If you stay at one of the better hotels, you'll hardly notice all the noise and bustle. And if you find yourself wanting to see the more traditional Crete, stroll through old Mália on the other side of the main road, where the taverna *Kalesma (daily from 5pm | Odós Omirú 8 | €€€)* still serves traditional Cretan cuisine. Lovers of ancient ruins won't want to miss the *Minoan Palace of Mália (Wed–Mon 8am–8pm, Nov–March 8.30am–3.30pm | admission 6 euros)* on the eastern edge of the town. It was the third biggest palace on Crete 3,500 years ago. 📖 *P4*

6 TÍLISSOS

15km / 25 mins from Iráklio by car

Would you like a romantic breather? Then head for the little-visited *excavations of three Minoan country houses (Wed–Mon 8.30am–3.30pm | admission 3 euros)* on the edge of Tílissos. The old pine trees will provide you and the 3,500-year-old walls with plenty of shade.

Flowering capers climb up the walls in the early summer. Cicadas

For many Cretans, picturesque Anógia is the most symbolic place on the island

will perform a private concert for you as you snooze in the grass. And once again, you'll be amazed by the exceptionally highly developed architecture of the Minoans: water pipes lead to the former two-storey buildings, feeding a cistern. Vast, lavishly decorated storage containers are dotted about, some of them still almost intact.

If you want to see how one of the Cretans' favorite foods – snails – is bred, visit the nearby *Snail Farm (daily 10am–6pm | admission 3 euros including coffee/tea/soft drink)*; the owners, Vásso and Stávros, run 30-minute tours of their property. Follow the signs on the road to Anógia. *M4*

7 ANÓGIA
43km / 1 hr from Iráklio by car

Where does the heart of "real Crete" beat? Most locals will agree that it's in Anógia, where they enjoy listening to the traditional Cretan music of the Xyloúris family. Widely regarded as the musical royal family of the island, the Xyloúris family hail from Anógia and their main home in the lower *platía* of the village is now a *museum (daily | admission free)*.

Across the square, young and old make themselves comfortable under mulberry trees in the 150-year-old, rustic *kafenío Míchalos (€)*, either with coffee and the semolina puff-pastry cake *galaktoboúreko* or with *rakí* and *mezédes*.

INSIDER TIP
One of the oldest *kafenía* in the country

In the minds of the Cretans, Anógia symbolises the resistance to the German occupiers in World War II: in 1944, they burnt the town down as punishment for the embarrassing abduction of their General Heinrich Kreipe to Egypt, and shot all the men they could find in the village. This is commemorated in a plaque and memorial near the town hall in the upper part of the village.

However, today one of the main reasons Anógia is considered the "heart of Crete" is because it is home to the island's biggest flocks of sheep and goats. Over 100,000 animals provide milk, cheese and meat, and they graze mainly on the common land of the uninhabited ⚑ *Nída Plateau* at the foot of the Psilorítis Mountains, which is reached by a 21km road. Many Cretans come to the tavernas of Anógia especially for the meat, particularly at the weekends. *Gagáris (daily from 10am | €€)* in the upper part of the village on the one-way street down is good. In this part of the village you will also find the information centre for *Psilorítis Geopark (psiloriti geopark.gr)*, and get hiking suggestions and free maps for Crete's highest mountain range. 🗺 *L4*

🟦 ZONIANÁ

43km / 1 hr from Iráklio by car

On the outskirts of the village is the 550m-long ✅ *Sventóni stalactite cave (April–Oct daily 10am–5pm, Nov–March Sat/Sun 10am–2.30pm | admission 5 euros | tel. 28 34 06 17 34 | zoniana.gr)*. Directly on the *platía* is the *Potamiós waxwork museum (summer daily 10am–7pm, winter 10am–5.30pm | admission 5 euros)*,

Today, the hippie caves in the cliffs of Mátala are uninhabited, but the cove is still a draw

with reproductions à la Madame Tussaud of important events in the history of Crete, from Minos to today. 🕮 *K4*

9 FÓDELE

29km / 40 mins from Iráklio by car

Interested in art? In this village in between orange and olive groves the painter Doménikos Theotokópulos was born in 1541. He later became known worldwide as El Greco. The home in which he was born *(May–Oct daily 9am–7pm | admission 3 euros)* has been wonderfully reconstructed. A lovely *kafenío* and a *church (May–Oct Sat/Sun 10am–3.30pm | admission free)* from the tenth century are in front of it. The church has a mosaic depicting fishermen at work. 🕮 *L3*

MÁTALA

(🕮 K7) **Today is life. Tomorrow never comes! That was and is the motto of the former fishing village of ⭐ Mátala on the south coast.**

During the Vietnam War, Mátala made a name for itself as a stronghold for hippies. Today the annual *Mátala Beach Festival*, which takes place around Whitsun, reawakens old memories. During the rest of the summer, hippie flair combines with day visitors and the usual holidaymakers. Now, the curious visitors scramble around the *caves (daily 10am–7pm | admission 4 euros)* in the rock wall on the north side of the bay that were once burial sites for the Romans and then, centuries later, homes for the flower children. In the few buildings and boat sheds on the south side of the old fishing settlement, people dine in good fish tavernas before enjoying the night in tiny music clubs. Between the two shores is a wide sandy beach some 200m long, and behind that a short bazaar alley that is still a little like a north African souk.

EATING & DRINKING

BISTRONOMY

This modern bistro, with its large roof terrace, is run by a Cretan family and a Frenchman, Jean Marc. From the smoked salmon starter to the spare ribs and the mango mousse, you're in for a treat! The Black Angus steaks are particularly good. *Daily from noon | near the end of the main street, opposite Hotel Zafíra | tel. 28 92 04 50 66 | €€*

MYSTICAL VIEW

The view makes the difference: you sit high above Kommós Beach here, over-looking Psilorítis and watching the sun sink into the sea. It's almost mystical. *Signposted on the road to Pitsídia, approx. 2.5km from Mátala | €€*

SHOPPING

AXEL GENTHNER

In the shop and studio of this gold- and silversmith who settled in Mátala long ago, you'll find original pieces of jewellery that no one else is wearing. Goldsmithing courses are also available. *Sun–Fri 1–7pm | main street, in the shopping area at the Hotel Zafiria | matala-jewellery.de*

BEACHES

KOMMÓS BEACH 🌴

Over 2km long and 40m wide, there's a taverna and the beach bar *Bunga Bunga* (popular with the locals) at the southern end, and a small town right at the north. Otherwise, you'll just find sand that you don't have to have bathing trunks or a bikini for. Unfortunately, it's 3km from Mátala, but then that's what mopeds are for.

MÁTALA BEACH

The beach for comfort-lovers, right in town. Full in summer, but relaxed.

RED BEACH 🌴

The red shimmering beach is a 30-minute walk from the village. Almost as far from civilisation as in the old hippie days.

FESTIVALS

MÁTALA BEACH FESTIVAL 🚩

Every year, at the beginning of July, the village hosts three days of 🐷 free live music, right on the beach. The colourful event has a nostalgic, hippie vibe. On the Sunday before the festival, Mátala's streets become a vast canvas for street art by participants aged from two to 102! *matalabeach festival.org*

NIGHTLIFE

BOHO BEACH BAR

A chilled-out boho beach bar, with loud music, that's popular with locals as well as tourists. Settle onto one of the large cushions and enjoy a cocktail with your feet in the sand. *Daily from 9pm | south end of the beach | @ boho_beach_bar_matala*

LE MINIÓN

At sunset, this cute yellow-and-blue juice bar transforms itself into an intimate evening venue, whose speciality is Cypriot beer on tap. Shortly before midnight, it changes again, this time into an open-air beachside destination. *Daily from 10am | on the edge of the fishing district beside the last set of beach steps*

The foundations of the Minoan city of Festós

AROUND MÁTALA

10 PITSÍDIA

4km / 10 mins from Mátala by car

Are you more the backpack type of tourist? Then the cosy *platía* of this little inland village is just the place for you. For generations, the *Café Synántisi (daily from 9am | €)* has been a meeting place for relaxed guests (who often bring their own guitar or lyre with them).

Those who appreciate good value and fancy something different should head to *Green Kukunari (daily from 10am | €€)*. In the restaurant's beautiful courtyard, southeast of the main street, Ziza and her team serve exclusively vegetarian and vegan dishes.

It's easy to hitchhike to Mátala and Kommós Beach, which is about 2.5km away. 📖 *K6*

11 FESTÓS ⭐

10km / 15 mins from Mátala by car

First Knossós, then Festós – that's the correct sequence for the two most significant Minoan palace towns on Crete. If you visit *Knossós (see p. 83)* first, you'll have a better idea of what Festós looked like 3,500 years ago – today all that remains are a few foundation walls. However, the setting is delightful, on a hilly plateau with views of the

In Míres people come to shop and chat

equipment from the last 200 years are beautifully arranged in cabinets labelled with exacting accuracy at the *Museum of Cretan Ethnology (April–Oct daily 11am–5pm | admission 5 euros)*. You will leave realising how much more comfortable our lives are today. ⊞ *K6*

13 MÍRES

13km / 20 mins from Mátala by car

INSIDER TIP
A must-see for market lovers

On Saturday mornings, this is where the region's farmers meet and take up (temporary) residence in the *kafenía* and fast-food restaurants, dine on souvláki and drink *rakí*. Street sellers have pomegranate juice and nuts for visitors, and the stalls sell all sorts of items ranging from imports from China to oil and fruits of the region and toys and kitchen utensils – anything and everything that will make a little money. ⊞ *L6*

14 GÓRTIS

19km / 25 mins from Mátala by car
The ruins of the island's Roman capital are on both sides of the road. On the north, they are fenced in and you have to pay to get in *(April–Oct daily 8am–8pm, Nov–March daily 8.30am–3.30pm | admission 6 euros)*. See the remains of the towering walls of the *Títus Basilica*, which dates back to the sixth century BCE, and the *Odéon*, a small Roman theatre for music and cultural events. Now under cover and behind bars are 12 of what were once 20 tablets of rules, carved around

Psilorítis and Asteroúsia mountains. If you want to save the admission fee, just go to the terrace of the excavation café, probably the loveliest on the island, plus you'll have close-up views of the Minoan town. If you are genuinely interested in Minoan Crete, then drive another 2km to the excavation of the tiny Minoan palace at *Agía Triáda (Wed–Mon 8.30am–3.30 pm | admission 4 euros)* in a shady little wood. *April–Oct daily 8am–8pm, Nov–March daily 8am–3.30pm | admission 8 euros | ⊞ K6*

INSIDER TIP
Lovely views

12 VÓRI

14km / 15 mins from Mátala by car
Traditional costumes and weapons, crafts, agricultural and kitchen

500 BCE. You'll learn a lot about the civil and criminal law of the time from these 42 stone blocks with 17,000 letters. Behind them is a meadow with an ancient olive tree, under which Zeus, the father of the gods, allegedly fathered Minos with Europa.

On the other side of the road (no admission) 🐗 are *remains* of countless Roman buildings, including an *amphitheatre*, the *Governor's palace* and a *thermal spa*. There are very few visitors, so you can enjoy antiquity in delightful peace and solitude.

If you're keen to find out more about Crete's history, then, as well as visiting Górtis, Festós and Agía Triáda, it's worth stopping off in Messará to visit the modern *Archaeological Museum (April–Oct Wed–Mon 8am–8pm | admission €6 | messara museum.gr)*, 1km west of Górtis, which opened in 2023. As well as interactive touchscreens in English, the museum has a free app, *MuseumMesara*, which you can download to access intriguing background information. Interesting exhibits found on the island lead visitors on a journey through time from prehistory to the Romans to the Byzantine era. Use the touchscreens to discover the possible meaning of the hieroglyphs on the Festós Disc (housed in the archaeological museum in Iráklio, see p. 78); admire the statues from Górtis and marvel at 2,000-year-old terracotta masks, which were probably used in theatre performances. 📖 *L6*

15 ZARÓS

25km / 40 mins from Mátala by car
This large town on the 340m-high southern slope of the Ída Mountains is well known for its trout farming and its many beautiful hiking possibilities. Two good trout *tavernas (€€)* are situated on the road to the little mountain lake of Záros. 📖 *L6*

SLEEP WELL IN IRÁKLIO

FRIENDLY & COMFORTABLE

If you're touring the island but don't want to compromise on comfort, then try the well-furnished *Hara Illios Village (99 rooms | Odós Agíou Panteleímonos | tel. 28 97 04 27 40 | hara-ilios.gr | €–€€)* in Káto Goúves. It's in the perfect location for excursions, and the friendly service will quickly make you feel at home. There's a relaxing garden with pool area and the hotel kitchen serves up varied menus.

SUSTAINABLE & ALL-INCLUSIVE?

For decades, the *Creta Maris Resort (680 rooms | Odós Dimokratías | tel. 28 97 02 70 00 | cretamaris.gr | €€€)* in Liménas Chersónisou has been proving that an all-inclusive hotel can be sustainable. This pioneering hotel offers loads of environmentally friendly activities alongside the facilities you could wish to find in such a large beach resort: numerous pools, bars and restaurants, a water park, sport and spa facilities and even an open-air cinema.

ÁGIOS NIKÓLAOS

PICTURESQUE RESORT AND GREAT OUTINGS

Shabby chic not your thing? Then Mirabéllo Bay should be the perfect holiday region for you. Even the Venetians once called it a "lovely sight". Everything here is beautifully looked after and spotlessly clean. Crete's tourism began here in the early 1970s: Walt Disney, Jules Dassin and Melína Merkoúri were among the first guests in the beautiful bay.

Countless hotels have been added to the early luxury establishments on the outskirts of Ágios Nikólaos, at Ístro and Eloúnda, where

In the evening, when the lights come on, everybody is drawn to the tavernas at Lake Límni

celebrities from all over the world like to come on holiday and even play golf.

Completely normal Crete awaits you in the hilly hinterland. There, you will encounter flocks of sheep and goats on the road, see the older generation sitting in the old-fashioned *kafenía*, as they have always done. On the Lassíthi Plateau, a mule might carry you up to the cave where the little-visited excavation sites of Lató and Goúrnia tell you about Crete's long history.

ÁGIOS NIKÓLAOS

⭐ **SPINALÓNGA**
A lepers' village built within the walls of a Venetian fortress ➤ p. 103

Λιμένας Χερσονήσου
Limenas Chersonisou

Αγία Βαρβάρα
Agia Varvara

6 Sisi

Μίλατος
Milatos

Σταλίδα
Stalida

Μάλια
Malia

90

Μοχός
Mochos

7

Αβδού
Avdou

29 km, 35 mins

If you find the high summer temperatures on the coast too much, escape to the Lassíthi Plateau where it's much cooler, especially at night. A pleasant night's sleep is guaranteed.

Κάτω Μετόχι
Kato Metochi

Μέσα Λασίθι
Mesa Lasithi

Lassíthi Plateau ⭐
7

Πλάτη
Plati

Άγιος Γεώργιος
Agios Georgios

Ψυχρό
Psychro

Καμινάκι
Kaminaki

Γαννίτσι
Gannitsi

CRETE
ΚΡΗΤΗ

45 km, 1 hr

MARCO POLO BUCKET LIST

6 ✓ Captain your own boat

Explore *Mirabéllo Bay* aboard a self-drive motorboat. ➤ p. 100

7 ✓ Party in traditional Cretan style

Join in the dancing on the village square at Mochós as part of a *Cretan evening*. ➤ p. 105

Do you prefer large pebbles to sand? Then the beach at Pláka is the one for you. The water shimmers in all shades of turquoise and there's a great view of Spinalónga. Just don't forget your beach shoes!

3 Spinalónga ★

Nisí Spinalónga

Kastélli
5

4 Eloúnda

1 hr

90

15 km, 30 mins

If you're staying in Ágios Nikólaos, you can take day trips by bus to various beaches – from Pláka in the north to Ístro in the south, you'll find a beach to suit all tastes.

6 ✔

Τάπαι
Tapi

2 Lató

● **Ágios Nikólaos**
p. 98

Almirós Beach

Ammoudára Beach

1 Kritsá

Κρούστας
Kroustas

90

Voúlisma Beach

Ίστρο
Ístro

Καλό Χωριό
Kalo Chorio

Gourniá ★ **8**

Παχιά Άμμος
Pachia Ammos

Πρίνα **9**

Μεσελέροι
Meseleri

Καλαμαύκα
Kalamafka

Μακρυλιά
Makrilia

Σταυρός
Stavros

4 km
2.49 mi

Agía Triáda Church: the contemporary mosaic above the portal is in classic Byzantine style

ÁGIOS NIKÓLAOS

(□ R5) **The little town that the locals simply call "Ágios" for short manages something of a balancing act: despite having more than 20,000 beds for visitors, even at peak season Ágios Nikólaos never feels like an overrun tourist spot.**

As the administrative capital for eastern Crete, Ágios Nikólaos is extremely independent and the atmosphere is decidedly un-urban.

The cafés on the shore of the small inland lake are only one centre; the streams of tourists are also drawn to the many cafés along the long coastal road that surrounds a rocky peninsula, as well as to the harbour front and the inviting shops in the pedestrian zone. Ágios (pop. 22,000) has developed organically, if haphazardly and not always imaginatively. The town is at its most beautiful on the shore of the small lake, *Límni Vulisméni*, which since 1870 has been connected to the town's harbour by a channel.

Fishing boats bob on the lake, which is surrounded by rocky cliffs on two sides. Here you will also find tables and chairs set out by taverna and café owners. Just as nice are the cafés up at the cliff top, where you have a view of the lake and the harbour. At night, the eastern side is the busiest. Mirabéllo Bay, with its many small bays and beaches, is ideal for exploring by boat.

SIGHTSEEING

AGÍA TRIÁDA CHURCH

Are these angels vegetarians? Possibly. The carrot in the modern mosaics above the portal to the main church could be a reference to the eating habits of the three little angels that Abraham and his wife Sarah are looking after. Or, on the other hand, to a preference of the mosaic artist.

The many large-scale murals inside the church tell other biblical stories, with more details for you to decode. If you know a little bit about the Bible, you'll have a wonderful time here. Unlike most medieval murals, these new frescoes in the traditional Byzantine style are easy to decipher. *Mostly 7am–noon and 4–7.30pm | admission free | ⏱ 15–30 mins*

ARCHAEOLOGICAL MUSEUM

Life was uncertain in ancient times. People could never be sure that the world would still be all right a year later, or that the soil would provide them with food. That is why they honoured fertility goddesses. And they imagined them to be like the goddess Mírtos, who you can see in the Archaeological Museum. Her insignificant head sits on a long, phallic neck. She has two prominent breasts and a (painted) triangle for her pubic area, while her spindly arms fade into insignificance. Also interesting is a clay house model illustrating how people lived here around 3,250 years ago. The fact that, , in the first century CE, they believed in life after death is confirmed by a very special skull that is displayed here as it

was found: surrounded by a wreath of thin golden leaves and with a coin in its mouth. The deceased needed this to pay Charon, the ferryman on the river to the kingdom of the dead. *Wed–Mon 8.30am–3.30pm | admission 6 euros | Odós Paleológu 74 | agiosnikolaos museum.gr | ⏱ 30–45 mins*

EATING & DRINKING

KARNÁGIO

This popular tavern with a view of the sea is busy with locals, even in winter. Diners sit on colourful chairs to enjoy the huge menu, which includes delicious *mezédes* and meat dishes, served in large portions. *Daily from noon | Kon/nou Paleológou 24 | tel. 28 41 02 59 68 | karnagio.gr | €*

PÉLAGOS

The traditional *kaiki* (fishing boat) on the terrace of this classic villa indicates what is best here: the fresh fish that lies on ice for customers to view. You can enjoy it in what is probably the prettiest taverna garden in the town. The furnishings are colourful, while the grilled squid with honey and fennel is a tender treat. *Daily 1–11pm | Odós Stratigú Koráka 10 | €€€*

SE-MELI

A cosy, somewhat alternative *kafenío* in an off-the-beaten-track location. Attention to detail and friendly service ensure a convivial atmosphere. There's a *mezédes* menu and occasional live music events. *Mon–Sat from 5pm | Kíprion Agonistón 15 | tel. 28 41 40 11 70 | €*

SHOPPING

HOUSE OF BIOAROMA

The natural cosmetics on sale here are all produced in a small factory on the edge of town. As well as sustainable products containing essential oils derived from Cretan herbs, there are also spa treatments on offer, from facials to whole-body massages. *Odós Iosíf Koundouroú 6 | bioaromacrete. com*

KERÁ

Lovely shop with tastefully selected items (both new and old): woven articles, jewellery, marionettes and dolls from Greek workshops. *Odós Iosíf Koundouroú 8*

MARKET

A large weekly market takes place every Wednesday morning on *Odós Ethnikís Antistáseo*, which starts on the lakeshore.

SPORT & ACTIVITIES

Water-sports enthusiasts are drawn to *Amoúdi Watersports (Ammoúdi Beach | tel. 69 77 44 72 14 | amoudi watersports.gr)* on the northern edge of the city, where they can enjoy water-skiing, wakeboarding, flyboarding and more.

You can also hire jet skis and ☑ a 25hp motor boat to sail on your own, without a boating licence, provided you pass a brief training session.

INSIDER TIP
Become your own skipper

BEACHES

The most beautiful beach in town is the 120m-long pebble *Kitroplatía Beach*, about five minutes from the harbour. Along the coastal road to Eloúnda, on the edge of town, lies the more sandy *Havanía Beach*. Almost 1.5km southeast of the town, you will find the sandy ⁕ *Almirós Beach*, and, about a mile further along the road to Sitía, is the sandy 100m-long ⁕ *Ammoudará Beach*.

It is easy and cheap to get to ⁕ *Voúlisma Beach* in *Ístro* further to the east with the public bus service. Tavernas, deckchairs and umbrellas can be found on all of these beaches.

WELLNESS

For a perfect day of relaxation, head to the House of Bioaroma (see Shopping, above) or drive 12km to Eloúnda where you will find numerous luxury hotels with generously designed, expensive spas which are open to non-residents, provided that you book in advance. The spa in the *Blue Palace Resort (tel. 28 41 06 55 00 | blue palace.gr)* is particularly beautiful.

NIGHTLIFE

Mega discos are out; they no longer exist. In Ágios, people prefer to spend the nights in the many smaller bars along the road around the peninsula, between the harbour and Kitroplatía Beach. Plenty of dancing goes on, especially when parties are announced on the notice board and on Facebook.

ÁGIOS NIKÓLAOS

Map labels: Archaeological Museum · Kon/nou · Akti Stylianou Koundourou · Kolpos Mirambellou · Knossou Knossoú · Ethnikis Antistaseos · Paleologou · Market · Pélagos · Kerá · Yianni's Rock Bar · N. Plastira Nikolaou Plastíra · Karnágio · Aléxandros · House of Bioaroma · Themistokleous · Limni Voulisméni · Apostólou Titou · Epimenidou · Dimokratías · Perípou · Mich. Stakianaki · Kon/nou Stakianaki · Ammoudára Beach · Voúlisma Beach · Almirós Beach · Roússou Kapetanáki · Sof. Venizélou · Agía Triáda Church · Se-meli · Diimokratías · Epimenídou · Epimevídou · Gasou

100 m
109 yd

ALÉXANDROS

Music bar in a roof garden with a view of the lake, lushly decorated with flowers. Dance music for every age and taste, and the DJ will take requests. Drinks on offer include Spanish sangría and Greek champagne. *Daily from 8pm | Odós Kondiláki 1*

YIANNI'S ROCK BAR

Owner and DJ Yianni still plays his music on CDs. Let's rock! is his motto, and he's always happy to oblige with requests. Look beyond your immediate surroundings, and you'll see the sea. *Odós I. Kundúru 1*

PERÍPOU

This culture café high above the lake also sells CDs and books as well as being a sophisticated cultural stage.

INSIDER TIP
Culture and cocktails

Locals and tourists mingle from 10pm with wine and cocktails. The music ranges from Greek songwriters to hard techno. *Daily from 9pm | Odós 28is Octovríou 25 | FB: Peripou Coffeehouse*

AROUND ÁGIOS NIKÓLAOS

1 KRÍTSA

9km / 10 mins from Ágios Nikólaos by car

This lovely mountain village is sometimes completely overrun by visitors.

It has plenty of souvenir shops, cafés and tavernas to cater for them, as well as a jewel of Byzantine art at the bottom edge of the village right on the road from Ágios: the *Panagía i Kerá* church *(April–Oct Tue–Sun 8.30am–3pm | admission 3 euros),* with perfectly intact frescoes dating from the 15th to the 17th centuries. The dome in the nave does not show Christ as the ruler of all; instead, there are four scenes from the New Testament: Mary in the temple; the baptism of Jesus; the resurrection of Lazarus; and Jesus's entrance into Jerusalem on Palm Sunday. In the centre of the dome, four angels represent heaven. The prophets of the Old Testament who foresaw the coming of Christ are depicted on the lower edge. The pendentives connecting the dome to the nave show, as is often the case, the apostles Matthew, Mark, Luke and John, whose gospels spread the teachings of Jesus to the people. Even for those not interested in theology, the images of hell on the west wall will leave a strong impression. ▯ Q5

2 LATÓ

13km / 20 mins from Ágios Nikólaos by car

Once upon a time, princes had ruins built in their parks because it looked so romantic. However, on the green hill of Lató, history really was the architect. A small theatre, the foundations of an old temple, the tiny, ancient market square, a cistern, the ruins of old houses and the town wall are all

No mercy: in the medieval fort of Spinalónga, lepers were left to fend for themselves

that is left of the town that thrived here between the seventh and fourth centuries BCE. Today they are the perfect spot for a picnic. *Wed–Mon 8.30am–3.30pm | admission 3 euros | Q5*

3 SPINALÓNGA ⭐

1 hr from Ágios Nikólaos by boat or 25 mins from Eloúnda by boat

The Venetian fortress island Spinalónga *(Kalidón)* launched its tourist career as the "Island of Lepers": between 1913 and 1957, it was a leper colony. The afflicted lived among the medieval walls in total isolation in a village they built themselves; they were also buried here. Amongst the lepers were craftsmen and farmers, a hairdresser and even a priest; people married and had children. But healthy newborn babies were immediately taken from their mothers and sent to an orphanage on Crete. Apart from the sporadic visits of a doctor, the lepers had no medical care at all.

The road around the island is only about 1km long. The trip out by excursion boat is worthwhile not only to experience a slight shiver while visiting the island, but also because of the diverse coastal scenery. A tour with an English guide is recommended; the tour guides bring the past to life with their retelling of the island's gruesome history. *Daily boats from Ágios (20 euros), Eloúnda (14 euros) and Pláka (12 euros) | admission 8 euros | R4*

INSIDER TIP
Guided tours

4 ELOÚNDA

12km / 20 mins from Ágios Nikólaos by car

Blue-bloods and celebrities from all over the world often only know one place on Crete: unassuming Eloúnda. Leonardo di Caprio and Lady Gaga are only two of the big names that have holidayed here. Nowhere else on Crete will you find so many luxurious hotels of the highest (price) ratings so close together. Private pools and butler service are as much a matter of course as helicopter transfers and luxury yachts for day trips. But you wouldn't think it from looking at the place. The luxury hotels are unobtrusive, away from the village, and the better-known hotel guests prefer to remain anonymous. If you'd still like a look inside, but are staying elsewhere, then book a table in one of the (expensive) hotel restaurants, such as the award-winning *Dionyos* that showcases modern Mediterranean cuisine, or the more unusual Peruvian-Japanese *Blue Lagoon* both at the hotel *Eloúnda Beach (tel. 28 41 06 70 00 | eloundabeach.gr | €€€)*.

Ordinary citizens appreciate the 400m-long promenade, flanked by tavernas, from the tiny harbour to the dam on the large island of *Spinalónga* (not the same as the leper colony), which passes through former saltworks. In the flat waters, snorkellers can explore the remains of the ancient town of *Oloús*, of which there remains an early Christian floor mosaic right behind the *Canal Bar.* *R4*

5 KASTÉLLI & AROUND

20 km / 30 mins from Ágios Nikólaos by car

Looking for some peace and quiet? With its old Venetian mansions and artfully wrought gates and railings, this sleepy village is one of the most beautiful in the region. Its narrow streets are full of wild geraniums – perfect Instagram material. An alley lined with eucalyptus trees leads you into the neighbouring village of *Fourní*, where almond trees blossom at the end of March. Here at the village square María Sfiráki awaits you in her taverna *Plátanos (daily from 8am | €)* underneath an old plane tree, where she serves fresh salads and affordable dishes like rabbit or lamb's liver. 🕮 *Q4*

6 SÍSI

22km / 25 mins from Ágios Nikólaos by car

A pinch of Figuera on Mallorca, a touch of Norway and a generous dash of Crete – Sísi is an exceptional place. The centre is a mini fjord, where you can swim among the fishing boats. Palms reach up into the sky on the western shore, while on the other side people enjoy a glass or cup of something in the cafés and bars. At the western exit to the fjord is a small sandy beach, and to the east there are a few fish tavernas. Hosts Níkos and Michális at *Agístri (daily from 11am | €€)* are delightful. If you're not too bothered about the fjord, walk 1–2km east, where there are more sandy/shingle beaches. 🕮 *P4*

Turn away from the beach for once and visit the rural Lassíthi Plateau

7 LASSÍTHI PLATEAU ★

45km / 1 hr from Ágios Nikólaos by car

A day away from the sea can also be pleasant. Perhaps you'll find it so appealing that you'll make the spontaneous decision to spend a night in pure rural paradise on Crete's biggest high plain. It's certainly possible. From *Stalída (📖 P4)* on the coastal motorway, an excellent road winds up in generous bends to the foothills of the Díkti Mountains. A look back at the coast will amaze you: how delightfully small are even the big Cretan tourist centres Chersónisos and Mália, when compared with those on Spanish or Turkish coasts!

The first mountain village, *Mochós*, welcomes you with one of the prettiest village squares on Crete – and it's time

for your first coffee. Here, in the summer, the taverna owners organize atmospheric ✔ *Cretan village evenings (Wed from 8pm | €€)* with music and folk dancing. In *Krasí* you'll see the island's oldest plane tree on the square with the large Venetian fountain.

At the *Kerá Kardiótissa Monastery (daily from 8am–6pm | admission 3 euros)* you'll admire the icon of the Blessed Virgin Mary – a keen traveller: according to the legend, she was taken to Istanbul by Turks no fewer than three times, but every time she made it back home by herself. On her last flight, she allegedly brought not only the chain, but also the pillar that the Turks had chained her to. These can also be seen in the monastery: the chain on the icon in the church, and the pillar in the cloisters. Then comes the *Museum of Mankind (daily 10am–6pm | admission 5 euros)*. A former customs officer tells you, in a charmingly naïve way, how he imagines the development of mankind from the earliest Stone Age to the moon landing.

At lunchtime, you'll be at the top of the *Ámbelos Afín (📖 P5)* pass, where the eponymous restaurant *(daily from 11.30am | seliambelou.gr | €€)* has a delicious pork roast waiting for you. It is served with 🌿 potatoes from the Lassíthi Plateau. This plateau, which is surrounded by high mountains, is 10km long and 5km wide. More than 20 villages are arranged around the perimeter to waste as little as possible of the fertile soil.

INSIDER TIP
A hog roast

According to legend, baby Zeus was nursed by goats in the Diktéon Ándron stalactite cave

The drive from the top of the pass to the 800m-high plain takes only three minutes, and you'll be greeted by a few windmills with cloth sails. You can see them in old photos in all the tavernas up here: until well into the 1970s, there were thousands of these wind turbines on the Lassíthi Plateau, where they were used to draw up the groundwater. Now they have almost all been replaced by motor-driven pumps. The main destination for the many tourist buses up here is the *Diktéon Ándron stalactite cave (daily 8.30am–3.30pm, May–Sept 8am–7pm | admission 6 euros)* above the village of *Psychró* (□ P5). This was a place of worship from as early as the second millennium BCE. According to legend, it was here that Zeus was brought up by goats because his mother, Rhea, feared that his father, Kronos, would see him as a rival and devour him as he had Zeus's siblings. It is possible to ride up to the cave on mules. The cave is well lit but sturdy footwear is recommended. At the car park below the cave, it is worth taking a walk through the private *Greek Mythology Thematic Park (daily 10am–5pm | admission 8 euros)*, where the legends are told through well-detailed figures of gods, heroes and fantastic creatures.

However, as an independent traveller, Lassíthi has so much more to offer you. You can stroll through the peaceful, largely unspoilt villages, enjoy short walks around the fields, and just experience the pure rusticity. The *Taverna Villaéti (daily from noon | €€)* on the main road in the neighbouring village of Ágios Konstantínos serves various Lassíthian specialities made with local ingredients from the plateau. □ P5 taverna *Pitópoulis (daily from 11am | €)*, because host Dímitris is a well-known *lýra* player and will happily serenade you. Once a week (usually on Wednesday), he, or sometimes his son, spends an evening playing for locals and other guests. Food and music are well matched: both are authentically Cretan. 🕮 *Q6*

SLEEP WELL IN ÁGIOS NIKÓLAOS

GREEN OASIS BY THE SEA

Crete's first luxury accommodation was developed in 1963 on a small peninsula. If you can afford to stay at the *Minos Beach Art Hotel (129 rooms | Aktí Eliá Sotírchou | tel. 28 41 02 23 45 | minosbeach.com | €€€)* on the northern edge of Ágios Nikólaos, you'll be accommodated in a stylish bungalow or a luxury villa with private pool, surrounded by a large garden, featuring mulberry trees, palms, bougainvillea and carefully placed sculptures.

RUSTIC STYLE

Alíki has lovingly restored several stone houses in the ancient and otherwise unremarkable village of Ágios Konstantínos, using traditional techniques to preserve their open fires and original features. *Vasilikata (9 rooms | tel. 69 77 24 84 56 | vasilikata.gr | €–€€)* is the ideal location from which to explore the peaceful Lassíthi Plateau in more depth. Products from the family farm are served at breakfast.

🞰 GOURNIÁ ★

19km / 25 mins from Ágios Nikólaos by car

On the coastal road on a low hill above the Gulf of Mirabéllo are the excavations of the Minoan city of Gourniá. The foundation walls of the 3,500-year-old houses are in good condition, and parts of the stairways that led to the upper floor can still be seen. Narrow, paved alleys lead to the former palace on the top of the hill. *Wed–Mon 8.30am–3.30pm | admission 3 euros | 🕮 R6*

🞱 PRÍNA

19km / 30 mins from Ágios Nikólaos by car

INSIDER TIP
A musical bonus

Would you like a private concert? Then make sure your MARCO POLO guide is clearly visible on your table at the

IERÁPETRA

A TOUCH OF AFRICA

Arabic music mixes with Cretan sounds on the radio. Winds from the south blow in dust from the Sahara every now and then. In the centre of old town Ierápetra, a minaret towers upwards. There are hints of northern Africa everywhere in the landscape.

Ierápetra and its surroundings are an unusual part of Crete, completely different from the other parts of the island. It can suffer from excessive heat in the summer, but it is an ideal holiday

Chrisí has fabulous sandy beaches, turquoise sea and nothing else – how relaxing!

destination during the spring, autumn and winter. You can swim in the Libyan Sea even during December and January.

The only area well developed for tourism is between Mírtos and Makrígialos; the remaining coastal resorts are far from the main roads and are sought out by independent tourists. Beach idylls are provided by the islands of Chrisí and Koufonísi off the south coast, which attract excursion boats in summer. Both are uninhabited; they have the finest sandy beaches and no hotels or tavernas at all.

IERÁPETRA

Kritikó

Nisí Día

Αγία Πελαγία
Agia Pelagia

Αχλάδα
Achlada

Παλαιόκαστρο
Paliokastro

Ηράκλειο
Iráklio

Γούρνες
Gournes

Λιμένας Χερσονήσου
Limenas Chersonisou

Δαμάστα
Damasta

Γάζι
Gazi

Καρτερός
Karteros

Χερσόνησος
Hersonissos

Μάλι
Malia

Γωνιές
Gonies

Τύλισσος
Tilissos

Κνωσσός
Knossos

Μοχός
Mochos

Τζερμιάδο
Tzermiado

Κάτω Ασίτες
Kato Asites

Δαφνές
Daphnes

Αρχάνες
Archanes

Καστέλι
Kasteli

Ζαρός
Zaros

Θραψανό
Thrapsano

Μαθιά
Mathia

Άγιος Γεώργιος
Agios Georgios

Παρθένι
Partheni

Αγία Βαρβάρα
Agia Varvara

Αρκαλοχώρι
Arkalohori

CRETE
ΚΡΗΤΗ

Άγιοι Δέκα
Agii Deka

Λιγόρτυνος
Ligortinos

Γαρίπα
Garipa

Άνω Βιάννος
Ano Viannós

Ασήμι
Asimi

Δεμάτι
Demati

Στέρνες
Sternes

Πύργος
Pyrgos

Άγιος Κύριλλος
Agios Kyrillos

Καστρί
Kastri

Άρβη
Arvi

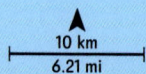

9 Léndas ⭐

Diskos Beach

135 km, 2½ hrs 🚗

Livikó

10 km
6.21 mi

MARCO POLO HIGHLIGHTS

★ **KAPSÁ MONASTERY**
A monastery in a lovely setting on a cliff above the south coast ➤ p. 116

★ **LÉNDAS**
Perfect for reliving the heyday of backpacker tourism ➤ p. 117

MARCO POLO BUCKET LIST

8 ✓ Take a boat to the beach

On uninhabited *Koufonísi*, you can bathe at dream beaches with an ancient theatre as your backdrop. ➤ p. 115

P é l a g o s

Μίλατος
Milatos

Nisí Spinalónga

Ελούντα
Elóunta

Σητεία
Sitia

Σκοπή
Skopi

Άγιος Νικόλαος
Agios Nikolaos

Crete is just 15km wide at its narrowest point, which means you can be on the north coast in just 15 minutes by car from Ierápetra. Escape potential boredom in the sleepy south by visiting Mirabéllo Bay and Ágios Nikólaos for a change of scene.

Makrigíalos is the perfect place from which to explore this part of the island. It's a manageably small resort with accommodation right on the beach.

Πισκοκέφαλο
Piskokefalo

Καλό Χωριό
Kalo Chorio

Σταυροχώρι
Stavrochori

7km, 2 hrs

Λιθίνες
Litines

5 Péfki

40 km, 50 mins

Ζήρος
Ziros

Μύθοι
Mithi

Stausee von
Bramianá **7**

Schmetterlingsschlucht **2**

3 Makrígialos

Γρα Λυγιά
Gra Lygia

East Beach
Ierápetra
p. 112

Φέρμα
Ferma

Κουτσουράς
Koutsouras

6 Kapsá Monastery ★

8 Mírtos

Καλό Νερό
Kalo Nero

8 ✓

Koufonísi **4**

Nisí Koufonísi

1 Chrisí

Nisí Chrisí

If you're planning an excursion to Chrisí or Koufonísi, check with the provider the day before your trip to make sure that the boat is definitely scheduled to depart and that the trip won't be affected by bad weather.

P é l a g o s

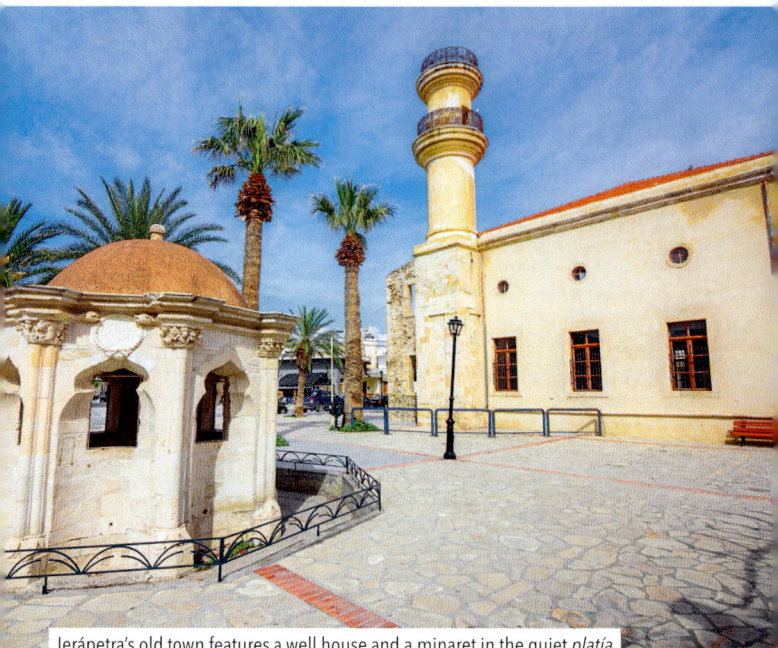

Ierápetra's old town features a well house and a minaret in the quiet *platía*

IERÁPETRA

(🗺 R6) **In the beauty pageant of Cretan towns, Ierápetra (pop. 24,700) is happy to come last. There are other interests here. All that counts is vegetable cultivation; beach tourism is a side-show.**

Back in 1965, Paul Cooper from Holland introduced the farmers to the cultivation of cucumbers and tomatoes in greenhouses. Local farmers became the richest in the whole of Greece. Even today, the plastic-covered *thermokípia* reach as far as the outskirts of Ierápetra. Almost every vehicle in the little town is a pick-up, because being the shopping centre for the farmers is Ierápetra's main function.

SIGHTSEEING

ARCHAEOLOGICAL MUSEUM

If you've succumbed to the Minos virus or make pottery yourself, then you'll enjoy visiting this little museum in what was once a Turkish school. It has two Minoan potter's wheels and a lovely Minoan sarcophagus with hunting scenes. The section with three Minoans in a cart that is being pulled by animals is very unusual. The cart is on spoked rather than disc wheels – and we're talking more than 3,300 years ago! *Wed–Mon 8.30am–3pm | admission 3 euros | Odós Ethnikís*

Antistáseos, close to the square in the new town | ⏱ *10–20 mins*

OLD TOWN

Ierápetra is no Greek idyll. But at least there is a very quiet quarter, where the town's Turkish population lived until 1913. You can easily spend an hour strolling around there. Start at the western end of the beach promenade. There is a *tiny fortress (currently closed for renovation)* that was built by the Venetians in 1626 with views from the battlements of the old town and harbour. Then make your way to the minaret you just spotted. It belongs to a permanently locked *mosque* with a well house on its square that has been restored. Then stroll back to the beach promenade, where a discreet signpost next to the *Levante* taverna indicates the *Napoleon House*. You can't go inside, but do look at it from the outside. It is said that Napoleon spent a night here in 1798 prior to his foray into Egypt.

EATING & DRINKING

BAKALÓGATOS

Modern Cretan cuisine served in convivial surroundings.

INSIDER TIP
Lovely group venue

Great for groups who want to order vast quantities of *mezédes.* Book in advance! *Daily from 7pm | Odós O Lakérda 13 | tel. 28 42 02 42 77 | €€*

LEVANTE

When the lovely smell of freshly grilled fish streams out of the kitchen, it practically pulls the sun-worshippers on the beach outside this restaurant off their towels. Vegetarians will also find plenty to enjoy in the friendly, rather chic taverna.

Host Níkos thinks his moussaká – fresh from the oven – is the best.

INSIDER TIP
Delicious moussaká

Daily from 11am | Odós Stratigoú Samouíl 38 | levante-taverna.gr | €€

SCHEDÍA

White taverna by the sea, 20m from a beach, on the outskirts of the town in the direction of Sitía. Many of the locals are regulars who appreciate the authentic Cretan cuisine and excellent value for money. *Daily from 1pm | east of the hotel Petra Mare | €–€€*

SHOPPING

MARKET (LAIKÍ AGORÁ)

How farmers shop: the Saturday market in the east of the town is not aimed at tourists. *Odós Psilináki*

SPORT & ACTIVITIES

Ierápetra Watersports (tel. 69 44 76 65 07 | FB: ierapetra watersports), a water-sports school on Ierápetra's beach by the big Petra Mare hotel, offers courses in windsurfing, water-skiing, sailing and diving; canoes and paddle boats can also be hired.

BEACHES

There is a short sand-and-gravel beach in front of the many tavernas between the harbour and fortress. Considerably longer is the 🦋 *East Beach* which begins at the Hotel Petra Mare and stretches for miles to the east. Numerous other beaches, mainly to the east, where a number of luxury hotels have been established in recent years, can be accessed by regular bus services.

WELLNESS

The best wellness centre is *Kallísti Spa (Katharádes | tel. 28 42 02 57 11 | FB: ostriahotel.gr/spa)* in the Óstria resort 5km to the east of the town by the beach. It is also open to non-hotel residents.

NIGHTLIFE

The cafés and bars along the beach promenade, such as *Caravan (Odós Kírva 15 | FB: CaravanCocktailBar)* are at their liveliest before midnight. After midnight, revellers head to *Privilege (Odós Kirva 14 | @saxo_3levels)*, with its rooftop and regular popular events. Locals also like to drive into the villages in the evenings: in Vainiá, 5km further inland, you can enjoy local wine and Cretan *mezédes* in *Tou Koutoúzou to Koutoúki (Tue–Sun)* on the village square.

AROUND IERÁPETRA

1 CHRISÍ ISLAND
50 mins from Ierápetra by boat

The island of Chrisí is perfect for a day in the sun. There are long, white, sandy beaches and dunes above which the bizarre roots and branches of the 10m-high prickly juniper trees tower. Until recently, excursion boats docked on the island, landing thousands of holidaymakers every day. Now, to protect the island's habitat, you can swim to the beach from the excursion boat or be taken ashore in a dinghy. You are no longer allowed to explore the interior of the island. *Cretan Daily Cruises (38 euros | cretandailycruises.com).* 📖 Q–R8

2 DASAKI BUTTERFLY GORGE
20km / 30 mins from Ierápetra by car

In good shape and up for a spot of climbing and stream crossing? Your enjoyable endeavours will be rewarded by large numbers of butterflies and a few small waterfalls. You'll need good shoes and plenty of drinking water – a towel is also useful in case you miss your footing and fall in. There's no destination; you just turn back when you feel like it: take a picnic with you. The walk starts at the car park 1km to the west of the village of *Koutsoúra (Park of Koutsoúra* or *Butterfly Gorge* on the signs). You can walk the gorge between May and November. 📖 S6

Sail to Koufonísi to bathe in the sea and contemplate the beauty of nature

3 MAKRÍGIALOS

24km / 35 mins from Ierápetra by car

The village street is superfluous if you holiday here. Just follow the miles-long 🏖 *Makrígialos Beach*, and eventually you'll end up at almost every taverna in the village and, above all, at the harbour, where the excursion boat leaves for Koufonísi. A tasteful selection of ceramics from Greece as well as good costume jewelry can be found in *Anémi* on the village street. Walnut cake and lemon tart are served in the small, photogenic *Café Ílios* right on the short waterfront promenade. The beach is fringed by tamarisks that provide shade, and you'll be perfectly comfortable among the boats in the taverna *To Stéki tou Miná (Mina's Place) (daily from 9am | €)*, which is also frequented by the fishermen. The only reason you'll have to go inland is to humour your inner passion for history. In the centre of Makrígialos, close to the village church and behind a fence, lie the foundations of an ancient Roman villa from the first century CE. Just outside the village in the direction of Ierápetra a brown roadsign shows the way to the remains of a late Minoan villa. 🗺 *S6*

4 KOUFONÍSI ✓

80 mins from Makrígialos by boat

The ancient Romans bred purple snails on the island to produce a dye that they used to colour the emperor's robes. In those days, Koufonísi even had a small, ultra-rich town with its own theatre. Now, like every other ancient building, it is slowly sinking into the sand, which adds the perfect

A monk from Kapsá Monastery

finishing touch to the island's charms. Apart from that, the only thing to do here is to swim off any of its 36 white beaches with extremely fine sand, and where the water shimmers in flat bays in every imaginable shade of blue and turquoise. In summer, the boat trips by *Cretan Unique Cruises (cretanuniquecruises.gr)* to Koufonísi leave almost daily from Makrígialos. 🕮 *U7*

5 PÉFKI

28km / 40 mins from Ierápetra by car
You go to Péfki if you're staying close by or happen to be driving through. Why? For a pleasant visit to the excellent, cosy *kafenío (daily from 9am | €)* in the village centre. At the front you sit under vine tendrils, at the back you have views of a gorge that goes into

the sea. The hosts put *rakí*, wine, cheese and olive on the table, cook a hearty omelette, and in summer also serve a small selection of dishes of the day. Two hours spent here amount to pure perfection. 🕮 *T6*

6 KAPSÁ MONASTERY ⭐

46km / 1 hr from Ierápetra by car
It's unusual to find monasteries right beside the sea. This one is in a particularly lovely spot: it was built in the 15th century, partly into a rock face. There are few visitors, and the peace is heavenly, including on the tiny shingle beach with old tamarisks just below the monastery. *Daily from 8am–noon and 4–7pm.* 🕮 *T6*

7 BRAMIANÁ RESERVOIR

5km / 10 mins from Ierápetra by car
Built in 1986, this reservoir at *Gra Ligiá* has a capacity of 16 billion litres of water and is the second largest in Crete. It irrigates the many greenhouses in the region. During the winter it is a bird paradise attracting more than 200 species. These include spotted eagles, snake eagles, peregrine falcons, bitterns, herons, pink flamingos and ibis. You can hike around the whole reservoir and there are observation points for amateur ornithologists. 🕮 *Q–R6*

8 MÍRTOS

15km / 20 mins from Ierápetra by car
It is said that the wind hardly ever blows in Mírtos. And the coarse sand on the long beach doesn't stick to the skin. It's impossible to get lost in this hamlet; you can't miss a thing on the

short beach promenade. If you holiday here, it's because you want to swim, swim and swim some more – and not have to choose from too many cafés, bars and tavernas in the evenings.

Still, should you suddenly long for activity, there are two archaeological sites that are within walking distance (sturdy shoes required). Close to the village, on the hills of *Foúrnu Korifí* and *Pírgos*, archaeologists have uncovered the remains of an early Minoan villa with about 90 rooms and a double-storey building from the New Palace period. Both sites are open to visitors and can be reached by following the brown signs on the coastal road from Ierápetra. It is only possible to get there on foot and both ascents start directly at their respective signpost. *Q6–7*

9 LÉNDAS ⭐

90km / 2 hrs from Ierápetra by car

Avoiding mass tourism has always been the watchword for backpacking tourists. Yet they've been coming here themselves in droves for 50 years now, without ever noticing that they, too, have become a mass. Be that as it may, this isolated little place on the south coast takes excellent care of its visitors, leaving many things as they have been for years. Today, though, guests no longer stay in the grandparents' emptied-out bedrooms or huts, but in modern guestrooms and studios; they still hold hands in the cosy beach tavernas, ==swim naked on 🏖 Dískos Beach== and drink wine on terraces right over the water. History has

INSIDER TIP
Like Adam and Eve

even left a little bit of culture: on the outskirts of the village are the ruins of a *Roman shrine to Asclepius (Wed–Mon 8.30am–3.30pm | admission free)*, the god of medicine. This coastal village, which is popular among young independent travellers and campers only has a few houses and tavernas. The whitewashed houses are surrounded by beautiful flower gardens and there is a short sand and pebble beach from where you can hire boats. *L7*

SITÍA

PALM TREES, LEMONS, RAISINS

East and west are more than just directions on Crete. They're world views. Both extremes of the island have their loyal fans. By far the majority prefer the west. The far east is extreme in a different way: no high mountains, but plenty of appealing, African-style landscapes, rich red soil, small canyons, stony plains and a few palm trees. The towns are insignificant and relatively new. What count are the quaint villages and often unusual beaches.

The palm grove beach of Vái sometimes becomes a victim of its own success

The region is still undiscovered by mass tourism. Only Sitía, which is the lively rural centre of the region, has a hotel that is slightly larger. There are only a few beaches around here, but they are very long and, apart from Vái, always have lots of space. There are only a few important historical sites too, and the Minoan palace of Káto Zákros sees more turtles than visitors. Like the other regions, the sound of the *lýra* can still be heard, especially at festivals, where the instrument lies ready for use in many a taverna.

SITÍA

MARCO POLO HIGHLIGHTS

★ **KÁTO ZÁKROS**
Between a beach and a rocky wilderness
lies a Minoan palace worth seeing
➤ p. 127

★ **XERÓKAMBOS**
Hardly anyone has discovered these
lovely beaches yet ➤ p. 128

MARCO POLO BUCKET LIST

9 ✔ Fresh fish and a sea view –
that's it!

Enjoy fresh fish in a perfect location on
Chióna Beach and forget all about the
wider world. ➤ p. 127

Faneroménis
Monastery **10**

Nisí Psíra

75 km, 1¾ hrs

12 Móchlos

Μυρσίνη
Myrsini

11 Chamési

Κιμουριώτης
Kimouriotis

Έξω Μουλιανά
Exo Mouliana

Παρασπόρι
Parasapori

Αχλαδία
Achladia

Looking for an idyllic
fishing village? Móchlos
can be reached in
around 40 minutes by
car from Sitía, Ágios
Nikólaos and Ierápetra.

Σκορδίλο
Skordilo

Μαρωνία
Maronia

Χρυσοπηγή
Chrisopigi

Κάτω Κρυά
Kato Kria

Άγιος Σπυρίδων
Agios Spiridon

Néa Presós

13 Thriptí

Ορεινό
Orino

CRETE
ΚΡΗΤΗ

Σταυροχώρι
Stavrochori

Άγιος Στέφανος
Agios Stefanos

Συκιά
Sykia

Λιθίνες
Litines

Αρμένοι
Armeni

Άγιος Ιωάννης
Agios Ioannis

Σχινοκάψαλα
Shinokapsala

Πιλαλήματα
Pilalimata

Φέρμα
Ferma

Γαλήνη
Galini

Μαύρος Κόλυμπος
Mavros Kolimbos

Μακρύ Γιαλός
Makrygialos

Καλό Νερό
Kalo Nero

L i v i k ó

Nisí Dragonáda

Nisí Gianísada

K r i t i k ó

P é l a g o s

Nisí Elása

3 Ítanos

4 Vái ⭐

If you're trying to find a beach without the crowds, set off early in the morning for Vái; if that beach is full, head north to Ítanos or south to one of the beaches east of Palékastro.

20 km, 25 mins

2 Tploú Monastery

● **Sitía**
p. 122

Palékastro **5**

Chióna Beach

1 Agía Fotiá

✓ **9**

10 km, 15 mins

○ Σταυρομένος
Stavromenos

Καρύδι
Karidi

Αδραβάστοι
Adravasti

○ Σίτανος
Sitanos

Ζάκρος
Zakros

6 Káto Zákros ⭐

Largely due to their location, Káto Zákros and Xerókambos are probably the least visited resorts on the whole island, which makes them perfect destinations if you're looking for peace and quiet!

◾ Chandrás plateau

Ζήρος
Ziros

Μέσα Απίδι
Mesa Apidi

7 Xerókambos ⭐

Ξερόκαμπος
Xerokampos

Γούδουρας
Goudouras

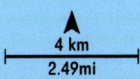

P é l a g o s

4 km
2.49mi

A shady place in the far east of Crete, a region that is perfect for independent travellers

SITÍA

(□ T4) **Sitía (pop. 15,600) could have been made for slowing down. It's unlikely that anyone here has ever experienced stress. A taverna's tables and chairs stand on the green strip of a four-lane highway – but the waiter is still the very picture of health.**

The town of Sitía starts directly at the east end of the beach promenade, where the cafés and restaurants draw all life to them. The shops that are important to the locals are all within a few metres of the beach *platía*; the alleys that lead up to the castle are all residential areas full of flowers and cats. Even the harbour of Sitía is quiet. There's a ferry twice a week, the occasional small freighter, and that's it.

SIGHTSEEING

ARCHAEOLOGICAL MUSEUM

Here's a young lad you should see! A Minoan carved him 3,500 years ago out of ivory from a hippopotamus. He chiselled his fine hair out of serpentinite stone, and originally his eyes were mountain crystals. His physical beauty was matched by golden magnificence: sandals, bangles, belt and loincloth were covered with gold leaf. You hardly notice that the pretty fellow is only 0.5m tall. *Wed–Mon 8.30am–3.30pm | admission 3 euros | at the town exit on the road towards Ierápetra | ⊙ 20–30 mins*

FOLKLORE MUSEUM

Anyone who wants to know how people in the region lived in the 19th century will gain a good understanding from the small folklore museum in Sitía. The period building contains a reconstruction of a household from the time, along with various tools from traditional trades and crafts. *Tue–Sun 10am–3pm | admission €3 | Odós Kapetán Sífi 26 | ⏱ 20–30 mins*

KAZÁRMA

The tiny castle dates from 1631, which makes it the oldest building in town. It hosts occasional concerts and drama performances in summer. *Wed–Mon 8.30am–3.30pm| admission €3 | northeast of the town centre, above the harbour*

EATING & DRINKING

CRETAN HOUSE

Located right by the water, this restaurant serves good, run-of-the-mill Greek cuisine – in large portions. The menu is extensive, and includes an excellent rabbit braised in wine from the Toploú Monastery *stifádo* and a scampi gratin. Also worth a try is the *skioufiktá*, home-made Cretan pasta. There's often live Greek music on Saturdays. *Daily from 10am | Odós Karamanlí 10 | kritikospitisitia.gr | €€*

MITSAKÁKIS

You'd better keep an eye on your calories in this confectionery which is the best in town. *Loukoumádes*, deep-fried pastries with honey and sesame are eaten both for breakfast and as a midnight snack, and the creamy custard pastry pie *galaktoboúreko* is a sweet dream. *Daily 9am–1pm | Odós K. Karamanlí 6 | €*

ZORBÁS

At Zorbás the tables are right by the water's edge. Meat dominates the menu and is served in huge portions. In high season, there are several barbecues on the go at once, cooking chicken, lamb, pork and offal on a spit. But you can also choose prawns or lobster, or just a regular pizza. *Daily 10am–1am | Odós Kazantzáki 3 | €€*

SHOPPING

ARÉTOUSA

Fancy something sweet? You'll get your money's worth in Anna Garefaláki's small pastry shop. Here you can find all the sweet specialities of the region – from *stafidotá* (pastries with raisins) to *xerotígana* (fried dough rings dipped in syrup) and *anevatá* (dumplings with *myzíthra* cheese). *Odós El. Venizélou 23*

MATTHAÍOS JEWELS

Matthaíos Markákis is from Sitía. He makes silver, gold and platinum jewellery that is inspired by Minoan and Byzantine originals. However, he also designs his own unique, often very playful modern line. Thanks to there being no middlemen, the prices are pretty reasonable. *Odós Fountalídou 1 | matthaiosgold.gr*

SPORT & ACTIVITIES

The town of Sitía itself is not recommended as a holiday destination for sports enthusiasts. The next watersport centre is about 25km away, in Vái.

BEACHES

The relatively stony town beach begins at the town's eastern edge. Long bathing days are better spent on the beaches of Vái and Káto Zákros which can be reached by regular bus services.

NIGHTLIFE

Fun parties with a good atmosphere often develop quite spontaneously in the little bars and *rakádika* along the harbour. However, there's no room for big discos.

BLACK HOLE

Thanks to its excellent cocktails, the Black Hole (seating inside and out) is always the number one venue in town.

Occasionally there is also live music. *Odós Karaveláki 7*

NOUVELLE BOUTIQUE

The audience is usually younger here than elsewhere and the music louder, thanks to the in-house DJ. *Odós El. Venizélou 161*

AROUND SITÍA

1 AGÍA FOTIÁ

7km / 10 mins from Sitía by car

If you're in the mood for a little archaeological expedition, take the bus or a taxi to Agía Fotiá. In the fields below the village, archaeologists have excavated an early Minoan cemetery with a large number of shaft graves and tomb chambers. A brown sign saying *Archaeological Site* shows the way. Continue about 250m on the dirt road until you reach the fenced-in excavation site on the low *Kouphóta hill* with ruins of an early Minoan settlement. As the beautifully prepared, EU-funded excavations are usually closed because of a shortage of attendants, you will have to look for a hole in the fence. That isn't difficult as there are several of them.

> **INSIDER TIP**
> **At your own risk**

On the way back to Sitía there is a small, bleak peninsula behind an old olive oil factory with the remains of the settlement of *Trypitós* from Hellenic times. There are no attendants there, either. ⊞ *U5*

2 TÓPLOU MONASTERY
21km / 30 mins from Sitía by car

In a move unpopular with some Cretans, the monastery's few monks recently leased large sections of this still completely unspoilt northeastern part of the island to multinational investors, who have plans to build Crete's largest luxury resort there, including several golf courses. Conservationists took the matter to the Supreme Court of Justice, but the monastery won. The landscape here may be "developed". Construction work has not yet commenced, so seize this opportunity to experience northeast Crete while it is still "underdeveloped".

The fortress-like medieval monastery is the only building for miles around, and is like an oasis in the midst of barren rocks and poor meadows. The *church* has one of Greece's loveliest icons, depicting numerous figures. It was painted by one Johannes Kornáros in 1770, and illustrates in many miniature-like individual representations of the text of a seventh-century ode entitled, "Thou art all-powerful, oh Lord!". Some people wish it would produce a miracle round about now.

Surprisingly unspoilt and pleasantly original is *Kamarotó (daily 9am–6pm | €)*, the taverna by the entrance to the monastery. The landlord is typically welcoming, but he sometimes feel the need to make sure that his guests respect the local eating habits: if he finds that you only have chicken on your fork, and no beans, he is going to intervene! *Daily 9am–6pm | admission 4 euros.* ⊞ *U5*

3 ÍTANOS
25km / 40 mins from Sitía by car

Bathing on the edge of the desert – that's what an hour on the beach at Ítanos feels like. Simple houses rise from the dunes. A signpost in the middle of nowhere names the hamlet as *Erimoúpoli*, which means "Town of Solitude". The sparse remains of an ancient town with two early-Christian basilicas are scattered around it. From the sandy beach with its crystal-clear waters, the view stretches as far as Cape Síderos, the northeastern tip of Crete, which the military has unfortunately claimed for itself.

Ítanos is a perfect alternative to the crowded, palm tree-lined beach of Vái, which is close by. There are no buses to get you here, no deckchairs on the beach and not a single hotel in sight for miles. *U4*

4 VÁI

25km / 35 mins from Sitía by car

Of all the beaches on Crete, the one at Vái is the most overrated. The fine sand beach adjoins Crete's biggest palm tree grove, although no one is allowed to go there. It became world-famous when it was still unfenced because many hippies preferred to camp here rather than be conscripted to fight in Vietnam. It still thrives on this fame, and every day during the summer, Vái now attracts more visitors than it can handle. The beach car park has become bigger than the beach itself. There are no hotels yet, but there are two *tavernas (daily from 9am | €)*, both of which belong to – yes, you've guessed it – Toploú Monastery. The water-sports station also has to lease its premises from the monks. But decide for yourself. If you find it all too awful, it won't take you long to get to empty beaches like the ones at Ítanos, Palékastro and Káto Zákros. *U–V4*

5 PALÉKASTRO

24km / 35 mins from Sitía by car

The large inland village of Palékastro has been lucky. It is so far from the airport at Iráklio that the major international organisers are not interested in it because of the long transfer times. But it has some wonderful

Off the beaten track: the village of Palékastro

beaches. This means that it attracts independent travellers. It's easy to get to the main beaches at Maridáki, Koureménos and Chióna, which are about 2–3km from the village square, on foot or by moped. There are several tiny bays to the south of 🐾 *Chióna Beach* which are mainly nudist. Wind- and kite surfers from all over the world meet on *Koureménos Beach*. The beach at Chióna has various excavations of a *Minoan town (Wed–Mon 8.30am–3.30pm | admission 3 euros)* and three excellent tavernas. You will struggle to find a more idyllic setting on Crete than that provided by the ✅ two tavernas located at the northern end of the beach: *Hióna* and *Fótis Seaside (both daily from noon | €€€)* have terraces looking out over the sea towards the Middle East.

Sandwiched between the village and beach, you will find Olga in her taverna *Kakaviá (daily from 10am | €)*. Olga has been serving mainly Cretan guests for over 50 years with her fish soup according to an ancient secret recipe given to her by a fisherman. At the *platía* of Palékastro visit the restaurant *Hellas (daily from noon | €)* which is traditional and unpretentious. At night it is the meeting place for locals and tourists alike. 🚇 *U5*

6 KÁTO ZÁKROS ⭐ 🐾
45km / 1 hr from Sitía by car

It's going to be an entertaining day – and that's a promise! If you're bathing on the miles-long shingle beach at Káto Zákros, remember there isn't a single piece of land between you and the coasts of Israel and Palestine,

about 850km away. That's vast. Káto Zákros itself consists of just a few little houses, loosely scattered over the coastal plain. It's hard to imagine anything more isolated. Just ten minutes away, turtles sun themselves among the ruins of the 3,500-year-old walls of a *Minoan palace town (April–Oct daily from 8am–8pm, Nov–March Wed–Mon 8.30am–3.30pm | admission 6 euros)* that once had 300 rooms – the easternmost one on Crete. From here, the Minoans travelled across the sea and traded with Egypt and other empires in the Middle East. They also had a copper-smelting furnace in Káto Zákros, the remains of which can still be seen here as one of the oldest industrial monuments in Europe.

Close to the palace, a path leads to the Valley of the Dead. Go past a stream and up into the mountain village of *Zákros*, just a two-hour walk away. The first third of the path is the loveliest. You walk through a forest of oleanders that are taller than a man, and can see the numerous grottoes and caves in the reddish rock faces where the Minoans and early Christians once buried their dead.

But Káto Zákros also offers modern art: the owner of the *Terra Minoika* apartments on the road just above the beach displays his interesting figures made of recycled metal and scrap. The taverna *Platanákis (daily from 10am | €)*, located on the road next to the harbour, serves particularly good food with a twist on the traditional Cretan cuisine. 🚇 *V6*

7 XERÓKAMBOS ⭐ 🌴

43km / 70 mins from Sitía by car

For many years there has been a paved road to Xerókambos, in the very southeast of the island. But it is still a secret hideaway for people who come in search of the many quiet beaches: small hidden bays in the east and the 50m-long, wide sandy *Ámbelos Beach* on the south coast. Sandy *Árgylos Beach*, with its cliffs of pure clay, is an unusual sight. There are a few isolated tavernas and guesthouses and a few umbrellas to rent. Between the beaches archaeologists have uncovered the ruins of a Hellenic settlement on a low plateau. 📖 *U6*

8 CHANDRÁS PLATEAU

31km / 40 mins from Sitía by car

The main reason for driving up to the Chandrás Plateau is a longing for a rural idyll. All around the village of Chandrás farmers grow quince trees and giant pumpkins. Energy is produced here with 18 wind turbines and many small solar farms. In August and September, grapes are spread in the village lanes so that they dry into sultanas. The enchanted and tiny hamlet of Voíla, near Chandrás, is magical all year round. Now deserted, it was once home to a Venetian noble family who eventually converted to Islam. In the chapel, which is always open (turn

Dolce vita on Crete: eat and drink in the shade by Káto Zákros Beach

the key to the right to enter), you'll find a mural showing the Virgin Mary with the baby Jesus above a tomb, and the local family in their traditional dress from the 16th century at her feet. The identity of the deceased is shown in a small mural: it is a young girl on her deathbed. The entire scene is rather touching. If you feel hungry in Chandrás, there are two simple *tavernas (€)* on the village square. ⌐ T–U6

9 NÉA PRESÓS
16km / 35 mins from Sitía by car
If you ever want to be all alone in an ancient Greek town, climb up the hill

that was once the site of ancient Présos. A few sheep and goats will keep you company, but travel groups or attendants are nowhere to be seen. There is not much archaeological evidence here, even though the hill was inhabited for 1,500 years during the entire Greco-Roman period. What remains are the foundations of a temple, a house and a few stone blocks scattered about. But what sticks in your mind is the memory of a remote spot in the mountains. *Freely accessible | access road 2km, well signposted in the village of Néa Presós.* ⌐ T6

10 FANEROMÉNIS MONASTERY
10km / 15 mins from Sitía by car
Fancy something unusual, but somehow typically Cretan? Then leave Sitía on the road to Iráklio and, after 2km turn right onto a narrow road signposted "Agion Panton Gorge". The road ends after about 10km at a small village that is inhabited in summer only for the wine harvest, and in winter for the olive harvest. However, the *taverna (€)* is usually open all year round – and usually without guests. Katerina, the landlady, is delighted whenever a guest does turn up and she always has supplies of fresh salad ingredients and vegetables. Just 50 steps from this unusual spot is a no less curious, long-since abandoned, small *monastery*. Probably founded in the 15th century, it is boldly positioned over the gorge. You can see a few remains of 17th-century frescoes in the sooty vaults of the church. Somehow, it goes perfectly with the general ghost-town atmosphere that prevails. ⌐ T5

🔟 CHAMÉSI

10km / 15 mins from Sitía by car

A spot for all those who love the beauty of simplicity: on a hilltop southeast of this traditional mountain village are the foundation walls of the only oval-shaped *estate (admission free)* from Minoan times. You can enjoy a magnificent view across the land and sea from a field full of fennel, aromatic thyme, sage and oregano. To get there from the western end of the village, turn left beneath the remains of two windmills onto a dirt track that ends at the excavation site after about 700m. 📖 *T5*

🔢 MÓCHLOS

30km / 45 mins from Sitía by car

You don't get to Móchlos by chance. There's rarely anything going on in the tiny village below the coastal road from Ágios Nikólaos to Sitía. And that is the reason you came here: to sit in the few tavernas by the water, bathe at the tiny beach – and perhaps go over to the uninhabited *islet* right off the coast. All life focuses on the *platía* by the water, with some sand and several tavernas.

If you haven't come to chill and read, you'll probably take a boat over to the bigger island to see the excavations of a significant Minoan settlement. The American archaeologist Richard Seager first broke the ground with spades here in 1908. The burial objects he excavated, including lovely gold jewellery, can now be seen in the museums at Iráklio, Ágios Nikólaos and Sitía. Work on the excavations was

The Faneroménis Monastery is abandoned; icons now adorn a rock cave next door

resumed in 1990. The only intact building on the island is the white *Chapel of St Nikolas*. Walk around the excavations, which have not yet been prepared for visitors, and you can look into several Minoan graves, see the remains of Roman settlements – including fish tanks – and traces of a Byzantine settlement. It's not particularly informative, but it is wildly romantic. Go to one of the tavernas and ask about *the boatman who is usually available from 1pm.* Warning: Don't try to swim over to the island, as there are strong, unpredictable undercurrents. 🕮 *S5*

INSIDER TIP
Resist the temptation

⓫ THRIPTÍ

50km / 90 mins from Káto Chorió by car

Vines are cultivated on the slopes of the 1,476m-high *Aphendís Kavousi,* in a landscape that resembles, perhaps, the highland tea plantations of India and Sri Lanka. Here, Crete's ancient character remains surprisingly unchanged. Winemakers live at the vineyards in summer and autumn to tend the crop. To reach Thriptí, you must travel by jeep from *Káto Chorió;* you can continue on mountain tracks to *Orinó,* with its many threshing floors and carob trees, passing through undisturbed mountain villages, such as *Skinokápsala* and *Ágios Jánnis,* before eventually reaching the southern coast at *Koutsounári.* 🕮 *S6*

DISCOVERY TOURS

Want to get under the skin of the island? Then our discovery tours are the ideal guide – they provide advice on which sights to visit, tips on where to stop for that perfect holiday snap, a choice of the best places to eat and drink, and suggestions for fun activities.

Hike along the coast from Agia Rouméli

DISCOVERY TOURS:
AN OVERVIEW

Akrotiri Spanda

Kolpos
Kíssamou

Kolpos Hanion

Chaniá ✈

90   E65   E65   A90   Souda

Kíssamos/
Kastélli

④

④   E75   90

Elafonissi

**A self-guided hike through
Crete's most famous gorge**

Liviko

Pelagos

20 km
12.43 mi

Gavdopoula

*Ormos
Almirou*

Akrotiri
Stavros

Kolpos Irakliou   Dia

Réthimno   90   E75

E75   A90   ①   Iráklio ✈   A90

Kolpos

Paximadia

Messaras

Anapodaris

Akra Lithinon

Liviko Pelagos

Kritiko Pelagos

Ormos
Almirou

Nature and history in the countryside around Réthimno

Réthimno

Akrotiri
Stavros

Dia

90

E75

Kolpos Irakliou

Iráklio

A90

Kolpos
Malion

77

3

77

97

97

Kolpos

Paximadia

Messaras

Akra Lithinon

Anapodaris

Kritiko Pelagos

Paximada

Kolpos
Malion

Akra
Aj.Ioannis

Dragonada

Gianisada

Elassa

Ormos Grandes

3

90

Spinalonga

Kolpos
Mirambellou

Psira

Ormos
Sitías

Akrotiri Plakas

Ágios
Nikólaos

Sitía

The beautiful surroundings of the Costa del Tourist

E75

90

2

Quiet villages between the Aegean and Libyan seas

Ierápetra

Akrotiri
Goudoura

Koufonisi

20 km
12.43 mi

Chrissi

❶ NATURE AND HISTORY IN THE COUNTRYSIDE AROUND RÉTHIMNO

➤ Discover a series of beautiful places, like charms on a necklace
➤ Marvel at archaeological sites while you walk
➤ Buy souvenirs direct from the potter
➤ Honour Crete's most important holy sanctuary
➤ Dive into a magical underworld
➤ Watch the sun set into the sea at the end of the day

📍 Réthimno

🔄 100km

🏁 Réthimno

🚗 1 day (2½ hrs total driving time)

ℹ Take a torch for exploring the ancient cisterns.

---

❶ Réthimno

10km

❷ Marulás

15km

❸ Arkádi Monastery

7km

VIA VENICE TO THE CRETAN NATIONAL SHRINE

You are advised to leave ❶ Réthimno ➤ p. 62 *via the old coastal road that runs east through the hotel quarter because there are no signs marking the improvised exit ramps on the motorway. In Plataniás, a well-marked road to Arkádi Monastery branches off from the coastal road. Shortly before you reach Ádele, take a little detour to the old Venetian village of* ❷ Marulás. A good portion of the historic houses here have been bought by foreigners and extensively renovated. Walk around the village for about a half an hour and then drive back to the main road. *As the road climbs upward, it passes through several villages and then through a narrow valley*. Almost unexpectedly, you will finally come to the isolated ❸ Arkádi Monastery ➤ p. 69, high up on a plateau. You should plan on spending about an hour looking around the most significant of the Cretan national shrines.

KEEPING YOUR EYE ON THE SUMMIT

An asphalt road leads from Arkádi Monastery east towards Eléftherna. At first, it still crosses over the plateau, offering picture-perfect views of Arkádi and the surrounding area from different points along the way. Drive through the desolate and barren maquis landscape, past grazing goats and sheep, before *taking the quiet road to the village of* ❹ *Eléftherna* ➤ p. 70. There are four quaint coffee houses in which at least a few chatty older gentlemen always seem to wait for new patrons to come in. The highest mountain on the island, Mount Psilorítis, can easily be seen from here to the southeast.

ANCIENT CISTERNS

As you drive on, you will come to the neighbouring village of ❺ *Archéa Eléftherna*, which stands on the site of the significant ancient city of Eléftherna. Systematic excavations first began here in 1985. To the left of the road, the archaeologists' findings are on display in the **Archaeological Museum** *(April–Oct Wed–Mon 10am–6pm, Nov–March 8.30am–3.30pm | admission 6 euros);* here, you can also enquire as to which parts of the excavations are currently accessible. From the village square with the very good taverna *Kafenío Filió (€)*, follow the sign to the **Acropolis Cisterns**, two huge cisterns that were carved into the

❹ Eléftherna

4km

❺ Archéa Eléftherna

4km

A dark history: almost 900 people blew themselves up in Arkádi Monastery in 1866

rock around 2,300 years ago. You can explore them carefully if you have a torch. If you *continue along the path to the north for six or seven minutes, you will come to a terrace* where you'll find the excavated ruins of a shrine of some kind beneath the old olive trees. This is the perfect place to enjoy a peaceful picnic accompanied by the natural music of the cicadas. You'll have to get back in the car to reach one of the other excavation areas of Eléftherna. *Follow the signs on the road to Margarítes that read "Ancient Eléftherna".* They will bring you to the remains of a Roman thermal bath and an early Christian Basilica.

AUTHENTIC FOOD AND SHOPPING

6 Margarítes ➤ p. 70 is the name of the next destination, which you should reach around 1pm. At the first potter's workshop on the right-hand side of the road, you can watch as man-sized storage vessels are made right before your eyes. The Cretans call them *pithoi*. A number of other local potters sell clay creations that are easier to take home on a plane. The two tavernas – **Mántalos** and **Giannousákis** – on the high street in Margarítes are equally good and serve fantastic food. *The route continues downhill until you come to the old*

6 Margarítes

10km

Watch potters transform sticky clay into beautiful vessels in Margarítes

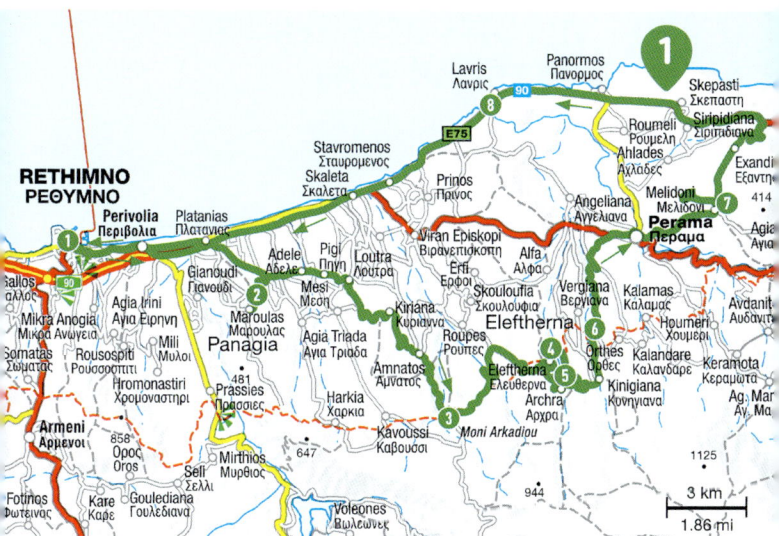

national road, which was the only link between Réthimno and Iráklio until the beginning of the 1980s. Turn right onto the national road in the direction of Pérama. When you get there, turn left towards the coast. You will rumble over a narrow bridge and then turn right just after the bridge to head to **7** **Melidóni** ➤ **p. 70**. Shortly before you reach the village, you can stop on the right-hand side at the **Paráskákis olive oil factory** and buy some good oil to take home. From the village square, you should drive another 2–3km in the direction of Agía because there are a number of charcoal kilns here. Afterwards, the village square in Melidóni is a great place to take a break before driving up to the **stalactite cave** ➤ **p. 70**, which is another Cretan national memorial site.

SWIMMING AT SUNSET

Depart Melidóni and drive to the sleepy hamlet of Exándis. Turn right onto the road leading uphill to get to the new national road, which you will then take to the west. Expansive **8** **Geropótamos Beach** is the perfect spot for a swim as the sun sets over the Aegean. When it's time for dinner, head back to **1** **Réthimno.**

7 Melidóni

18km

8 Geropótamos Beach

18km

1 Réthimno

❷ QUIET VILLAGES BETWEEN THE AEGEAN AND LIBYAN SEAS

➤ Let unspoilt nature work its magic on you
➤ Take a plunge into the cool waters of the Libyan Sea
➤ Watch the sultana farmers at work
➤ Go on a hike and discover ruins in the middle of nowhere

📍 Sitía

🏁 Sitía

🔄 90km

🚗 1 day (2 hrs total driving time)

ℹ You will need a car or a motorcycle/motor scooter for this tour

❶ Sitía

25km

❷ Dafní

10km

THROUGH DEEP VALLEYS

Depart ❶ Sitía ➤ p. 122 and *head south, following the signs for Ierápetra. When you get to Piskokéfalo, turn right onto the small road to Análipsi. After passing through Achládia, the road climbs up to the pass at Skordílo.* In early summer, gorse seems to bloom everywhere. Later in the season, it looks like the rocky landscape has been blanketed with puffy pillows of green herbs. At the top of the pass, you will get your first glimpse of the Libyan Sea. *Drive into the high valley of* ❷ Dafní, *which is full of olive trees. After you've left Dafní, you will come to another mountain valley further below.* In this area, you will see blocks of pure chalk lying on the side of the road. Get your creative juices flowing and draw a little picture on the road with one of the small pieces of chalk lying around.

As you drive on, you will come to the mouth of a valley that runs from the north coast into the mountains. Storms often blow through this natural wind tunnel, shearing through the pine trees. Over the next few miles, you'll notice how the winds have cut the most bizarre, lopsided shapes into the trees. *Drive through Chrisopigí and pass by the totally isolated mountain village of Lápithos, making your next stop in*

Map labels (as visible):

2 · 3 km / 1.86 mi

Ormos Mochlou · M. Faneromenis · Papadiokampos / Παπαδιόκαμπος · Liopetra 428 · Linares / Λινάρες · **SITIA** / **ΣΙΤΕΙΑ** · Kasarma / 90 · Kalavros / Κάλαβρος · Skopi / Σκόπη · Piskokefalo / Πισκοκέφαλος · Petras / Πετράς · Skalabiolakas · E75 · Amikou / Αμικου · Echo Mouliana / Έξω Μουλιανα · 2020 · Chamezi / Χαμέζι · Kimouriotis / Κιμουριώτης · K. Episkopi / K. Επισκοπή · Stavromenos / Σταυρωμένος · Tourloti / Τουρλωτή · Mirsini / Μυρσίνη · 90 · Paraspori / Παράσπορι · Abladia / Αχλάδια · Zou / Ζου · K. Dris / K. Δρις · Sfaka / Σφάκα · Messa Mouliana / Μέσα Μουλιανα · Riza / Ρίζα · Maronia / Μαρώνια · Sfakia / Σφακια · Prinias 803 · Platanos / Πλάτανος · O r o s · Skordilo / Σκορδίλο · Ep. Episkopi / Επ. Επισκοπή · Sandali / Σανδάλι · Katsidoni / Κατσιδόνι · Hrisopigi / Χρυσοπηγή · Oros Koprokefala 1179 · Epano Kria / Επάνω Κρυα · Ag. Georgios / Αγ. Γεώργιος · Ag. Spiridon / Αγ. Σπυρίδων · Kalamavki / Καλαμαύκη · Kato Kria / Κάτω Κρυα · Nea Presos / Νεα Πρωισος · Lapithos / Λαπίθος · **2** Dafni / Δάφνη · Romanati 937 · Sikia / Συκιά · Sklavi / Σκλαβοί · Pappagiannades / Παπαγιαννάδες · Aori / Αόρι · Vori / Βόρι · H a n d r a s · Stavrohori / Σταυροχώρι · Pefki / Πεύκοι · Handras / Χάνδρας · Voila / Βόιλα · **3** · 460 · Lithines / Λιθίνες · Etia / Ετιά · **6** · Armeni / Αρμένοι · 368 · Ag. Stefanos / Αγ. Στέφανος · Azail / Αζάιλ · 715 · Ag. Sofia / Αγ. Σοφία · Mesa Apidi / Μέσα Απίδι · Koutsouras / Κουτσουρας · Analipsi / Αναλήψη · Pilalimata / Πιλαλήματα · Spiti Minoa · **4** · **5** **Makrigialos** / **Μακρυγιαλός** · Pezoulas / Πεζούλας · K. Perivolakia / K. Περιβόλακια · Ep. Perivolakia / Επ. Περιβόλακια · Ag. Triada / Αγ. Τριάδα · 410

---

3 **Stavrochóri**. The excellent taverna **Stravodoxari** on the tiny, idyllic village square is the perfect place for a long-overdue coffee. *The main road ends in the coastal village of* **4** **Koutsourás**. Greenhouses have been built here right in the centre of the village – take a minute to inspect one of them up close.

HIKING ON NARROW TRACKS
Take the coastal road to the left and drive for just five minutes to **5** **Makrígialos** ➤ p. 115. After a swim in the Libyan Sea, the small harbour is an excellent place to grab lunch. *Then, follow the main road*

INSIDER TIP
Lunch with a harbour view

3 Stavrochóri

7km

4 Koutsourás

3km

6 Makrígialos

17km

east again. Just after Vóri, turn right and drive up to ⑥ Etía *and the village of* ⑦ Chandrás. On this elevated plateau, where sultanas are the main crop, the pace of life is leisurely and tourists are few and far between, as you'll notice in the village *kafenía*. Once you are ready to leave this tranquillity behind, take a small detour from ⑧ Néa Presós ➤ p.129 to the meagre ruins of the ancient city of Presós on a hill. You can hike along the narrow paths to your heart's content with the most beautiful views of the Cretan mountains. Late in the afternoon, *drive north to get back to* ❶ Sitía.

❸ THE BEAUTIFUL SURROUNDINGS OF THE COSTA DEL TOURIST

➤ **Have lunch in a peaceful farming village**
➤ **Swim through a fjord**
➤ **Visit a lonely monastery**
➤ **Observe craftspeople at work**
➤ **Visit a Minoan palace**
➤ **Enjoy family fun in the water**

⚲ Ágios Nikólaos   🏁 Chersónisos

→ 100km   🚗 1 day (2½ hrs total driving time)

ⓘ Bring a torch to explore the cave
The **Palace of Mália** is only open until 3pm

GREAT VIEWS AND COFFEE IN THE SHADE

Follow the coastal road from ❶ Ágios Nikólaos ➤ p.98 *northwards to Eloúnda and Pláka. Leave the coast behind and drive up to the mountain village of* ❷ Vroúchas. Enjoy the spectacular view of the fortress island of Spinalónga ➤ p 103. *Keep driving through the countryside* dotted with isolated small villages such

Get in the mood for the tranquillity of the Chandrás plain in the quiet village of Etiá

as ❸ **Káto Loúmas** and ❹ **Skiniás**. If you find an open *kafenío*, stop for a drink – the locals will be surprised to see a tourist. *At the fork just after leaving Váltos, take the road to* ❺ **Karídi**. Shortly before you get to the village, you will spy a road to the left leading to the **Aréti Monastery** at a height of 530m, which is worth a visit. In the 16th century, it once served as a bishop's residence. Today, only one monk lives here. You can then enjoy a coffee break under a plane tree on the village square at ❻ **Fourní** ➤ p. 104 *before you continue along a eucalyptus-lined road to the neighbouring village of* ❼ **Kastélli** ➤ p. 104. Spend a quarter of an hour strolling through the pretty village, which has numerous Venetian buildings.

CAVE EXPLORATION

Drive through Nikithianó to ❽ **Neápoli**, *and then follow the signs to Iráklio in order to get to Latsída. In the centre of the village, turn right and then just outside the village, turn left towards* ❾ **Kounáli.** Stop for an excellent lunch along the main road on the shady terrace of the taverna **To Kounáli** *(€)* owned by a former ship's cook and his flower-crazy daughter. A bit of exercise will do you good after your meal. *On the curvy road between*

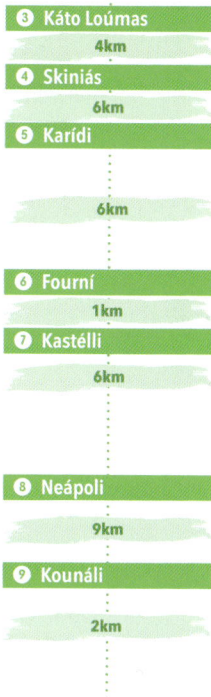

❸ **Káto Loúmas**	
4km	
❹ **Skiniás**	
6km	
❺ **Karídi**	
6km	
❻ **Fourní**	
1km	
❼ **Kastélli**	
6km	
❽ **Neápoli**	
9km	
❾ **Kounáli**	
2km	

Kounáli and Mílatos, park your car and take a short walk to the **⑩ Milátou stalactite cave** *on the left-hand side. Don't forget to bring a torch! After exploring this subterranean world,* *drive through Mílatos to arrive at* **⑪ Sísi ➤ p. 104** with its astoundingly beautiful, although extremely short, fjord. For a cup of coffee or a refreshing drink, head to the **Skipper Cocktail Bar** directly above the fjord. If you feel like testing the water, there is a small sandy beach on the western end of the fjord where you can go for a swim.

FROM ANTIQUITY TO WATER PARKS

As you leave Sísi, follow the signs for Mália and Iráklio, which will bring you to the motorway. After about 2km, follow the signs to the **Minoan Palace of Mália ➤ p. 86**. If you can get there before it closes (3pm), it's worth taking a look. If you're too late, you'll have to make do with a glimpse through the wire fence. You haven't wasted your time either way as the lovely beach and harbour of **⑫ Mália ➤ p. 86** are just a stone's throw away. Seafood lovers can try octopus stew, sea urchin or an appetising salmon tartare with avocado

The Minoans chose premium locations for their palaces, at Knossós and Mália

sauce in the *Malia Port taverna (daily from 11am | €€)*.
Afterwards, *continue to the west on the old national
road (avoid the motorway!) until you come to the resort
of Stalída on the eastern edge of* ⑬ **Liménas
Chersónisou ➤ p. 85**. It is home to the **Star Beach
Water Park ➤ p. 86**, with its bungee crane and a variety of water-sports stations. How about a little
parasailing adventure?

END THE DAY WITH A CRETAN EVENING

*Drive into the town of Liménas Chersónisou and follow
the signs for the village of* ⑭ **Koutouloufári**, about
1km above the main town, where plenty of jewellery
and handicrafts are on offer. For a late dinner, head to
the beautiful village square of ⑮ **Chersónisos ➤ p. 85**,
where several tavernas line the square's edges.

10km

⑬ **Liménas
Chersónisou**

2km

⑭ **Koutouloufári**

2km

⑮ **Chersónisos**

④ A SELF-GUIDED HIKE THROUGH CRETE'S MOST FAMOUS GORGE ✓

➤ Spend a night in utter silence
➤ Complete a hiking challenge
➤ Watch Cretan wild goats scramble around
➤ Marvel at the high peaks above the steep cliffs
➤ Cool down in the Libyan Sea
➤ Finish off the day with a boat tour

📍	Chaniá	🏁	Chaniá
🔄	150km	🚶	2 days (5–6 hrs total hiking time)
📊	medium		

ℹ️ It is essential to take water and sun protection. The gorge is only accessible from the beginning of May to 15 October. The last public bus from Chaniá departs at 7.45am. Bus timetables: *e-ktel.com*; ferry timetables: *anendyk.gr*

DAY 1
① Chaniá
37km
② Omalós Plateau
5km
③ Samariá Gorge
100m
④ Xylóskalo
7km

BRIGHT AND EARLY INTO THE GORGE

Make sure you're on time to catch the 7.45am bus from ① Chaniá ➤ *p. 44 up to* ② Omalós Plateau *because there is no later bus.* You will arrive around 9am and then treat yourself to a refreshing day of relaxation at a height of over 1,000m. Spend the night in the tranquil village of Omalós.

Start your hike through the gorge when it opens early the next morning at 7am. This way, you will have already done most of the trail by the time the heat really intensifies at midday. *A shuttle bus from your hotel will take you the few kilometres to the head of the* ③ Samariá Gorge ➤ *p. 55. The actual trail begins a few steps further at a height of 1,229m at the* ④ Xylóskalo, *the wooden steps that bring you into the gorge.* Don't worry, though, because these are not actually stairs, but rather a pleasant forest path with steps here and there.

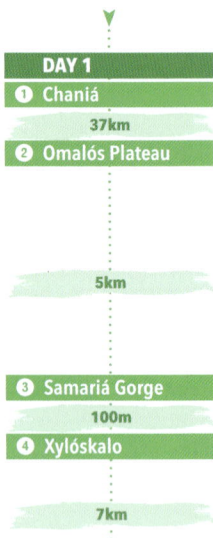

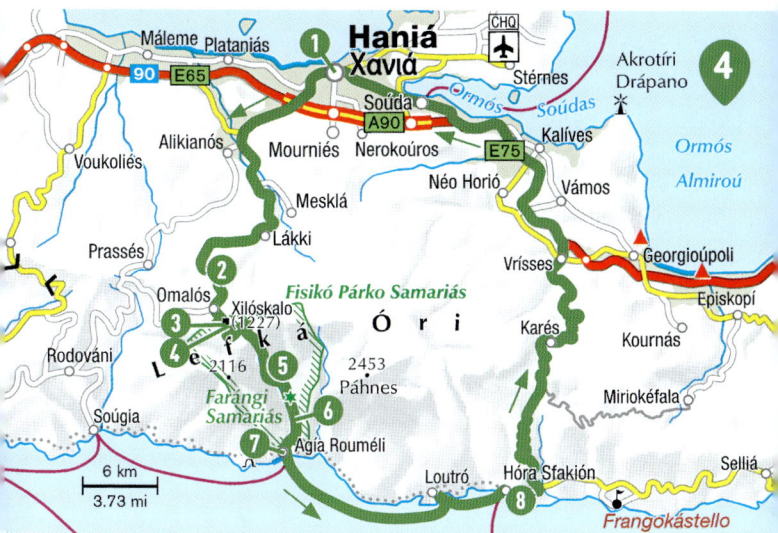

Under the eyes of the Gíngilos (2,080m), the trail wanders *for about an hour up through the forest to the floor of the gorge* through which a rushing stream flows. You will come to the abandoned village of ⑤ **Samariá**, which has a freshwater spring, a first-aid station and toilets. The last residents left in 1962 when the gorge was turned into a national park.

⑤ Samariá

THE SEA AND A BOAT AWAIT AT THE FINISH LINE

As the trail continues, the gorge narrows steadily until you come to the so-called ⑥ **Iron Gate (Sideróporta)**, where it is only 3–4m wide. *Shortly thereafter, the coastal plain will appear before you, and then it is just another 3km (without any shade) to the coastal hamlet of* ⑦ **Agía Rouméli** with its many tavernas, guesthouses and a long pebble beach. There is usually a shuttle bus to cover the last few kilometres to the pier, where the first thing you should do is buy your tickets for the ferry to Chóra Sfakíon. Then you can enjoy a long break in one of the tavernas and maybe a swim. The last ferry usually leaves around 5.30pm, arriving about an hour later. The ⑧ **Chóra Sfakíon** ➤ p. 56, the public buses to Chaniá always wait for the ferry to dock, so you should arrive back in ❶ **Chaniá** at 8.30pm.

DAY 2

55km

⑥ Iron Gate

3.5km

⑦ Agía Rouméli

19km

70km

⑧ Chóra Sfakíon

GOOD TO KNOW

HOLIDAY BASICS

ARRIVAL

+ 2 hours time difference

Crete is two hours ahead of Greenwich Mean Time, seven hours ahead of US Eastern Time and seven hours behind Australian Eastern Time.

GETTING THERE

There are daily flights to Crete all year with Olympic Air/Aegean Airlines *(aegeanair.com)*. Between Easter and October there are also many direct charter and budget flights directly to Iráklio and Chaniá, but these can sometimes be more expensive than normal flights. Flights from London to Iráklio take about three and a half hours, and from Athens about 40 minutes. At both airports there are taxis for onward travel. At Chaniá and Iráklio there are also reasonably priced buses to the nearby city centre. From Iráklio, there are regular buses to the eastern seaside resorts and to the towns of Ágios Nikólaos, Ierápetra and Sitía. Luggage storage is only available at Iráklio.

There is no direct ferry service from Italy. You have to cross to Patras on the Peloponnese first, then from Piraeus to Crete. There are daily ferries from Piraeus to Chaniá and Iráklio (6–12 hrs); several times a week to Réthimno and Sitía. There are also two to three ferries a week from Kíssamos on the Peloponnese.

GETTING IN

You can travel to Greece without a visa so long as your stay does not exceed 90 days. If you intend to stay for longer, check which visa you require with the

Expect more sheep than tourists on the Omalós Plateau

Greek embassy. On arrival, your passport must have at least six months' validity after your point of departure from Greece.

CLIMATE & WHEN TO GO

Crete is not really a winter holiday destination. Between November and March it can rain and be quite cool. The best holiday months are from April to October. Swimming in the sea is best between May and November. May is the most beautiful time to travel in Crete: it is very green and there are flowers in bloom everywhere. It hardly rains from June to September; temperatures can rise above 40°C and the average temperatures for July and August are 30°C by day and 20°C at night. There are also often strong winds on Crete that can bring the ferries to a standstill for hours even in the summer.

OFFSET YOUR FLIGHT

The return flight is likely to be the most environmentally damaging part of your holiday. A single traveller on a return flight from London to Iráklio generates nearly one tonne of CO_2. You can offset this emission at myclimate.org (and other organisations) for around £21. The money is used to fund climate protection projects around the world.

GETTING AROUND

BUSES

There are regular and 🐖 🐗 cheap public buses to almost every town in Crete and travelling by bus is recommended, since parking spaces are scarce. The blue buses only travel within municipal districts. Long-distance buses (often green) travel between Iráklio, Ágios Nikólaos, Chaniá, Ierápetra, Sitía and Réthimno. Tickets are bought in advance online or at the bus terminals in the cities; if you get on later, you buy the tickets from the driver. Tickets for city buses must be bought in advance at ticket machines, kiosks, hotel receptions and shops. Timetables and online tickets for western Crete can be found at *e-ktel.com* and for eastern Crete at *ktelherlas.gr.*

CAR HIRE

Cars, motorbikes, Vespas and mopeds can be rented at all airports as well as in the towns and resorts. Your national driving licence may be sufficient proof of identity when booking, but a credit card in the driver's name may also be required. It is highly recommended that you compare prices on the Internet. Usually, Greek rental firms hand the hire vehicle over with an almost empty tank. You are expected to return it in the same state and will not get a refund for excess petrol in the tank.

FERRIES

Ferries within Crete only sail along the south coast between Paleochóra and Chóra Sfakíon and also between the coastal towns in this region and the island of Gávdos. For schedules and prices please visit *anendyk.gr.*

ORGANISED TOURS

All holiday resorts and hotels offer organised excursions. Bus tours are usually accompanied by local and licensed guides. Gorge hikes and boat trips with transfer from the hotel to the harbour and back are often available.

ROAD TRAFFIC

The maximum speed in towns is 50kmh and on national roads 90kmh. Maximum blood alcohol level is 0.5. Right of way is not indicated as such. You will only recognise it by the "Stop" and "Give Way" signs on minor roads. At roundabouts, anything coming from the right has right of way, unless signposted otherwise. Cretans are notorious for cutting curves, so always keep to the right of the road. Also get used to honking at blind corners! During autumn, the roads are especially wet and slippery and care should be taken. Car rental firms often have contracts with private breakdown recovery services.

TAXIS

Taxis are available in abundance and are not very expensive. Get one at the taxi rank, wave one down in the street, or book in advance for a surcharge.

EMERGENCIES

CONSULATES & EMBASSIES
British Vice Consulate Crete
17 Thalita | Ag. Dimitrios Sq. | Iráklio | tel. 28 10 22 40 12 | crete@fco.gov.uk

Canadian Embassy (Athens)
48 Ethnikis Antistaseos | 15231 Athens | tel. 21 07 27 34 00 | canadainternational.gc.ca/greece-grece

UK Embassy (Athens)
1 Ploutarchou | 10675 Athens | tel. 21 07 27 26 00 | ukingreece.fco.gov.uk

US Embassy (Athens)
91 Vasilissis Sophias | 10160 Athens | tel. 21 07 21 29 51 | gr.usembassy.gov

EMERGENCY SERVICES

Dial 112 for all emergency services: police, fire brigade and ambulance. The number is toll-free countrywide, and English is spoken.

HEALTH

Well-trained doctors guarantee basic medical care throughout Crete although there is often a lack of equipment. If you are seriously ill, it is advisable to return home; this will be covered by your travel insurance. Emergency hospital treatment can be accessed if you present the Global Health Insurance Card (GHIC) available from *gov.uk*. Non-emergency treatment should be paid for in cash; get a receipt and then present your bills to the insurance company for a refund.

ESSENTIALS

ACCOMMODATION

A large number of hotels, B&Bs, holiday apartments and homes are available not just in the towns and coastal resorts, but these days also in many of the mountain villages. Almost all accommodation providers are linked with the *booking.com* portal where you can get a good overview. You may of course be able to book directly with the landlord if that's any cheaper.

Camping anywhere other than a campsite is prohibited in Crete. There are a total of 16 camping sites on the island that are open between April and October. In Crete there are several simple accommodation units calling themselves "youth hostels" but none of them is a member of the international Youth Hostel Association. They are mostly privately owned. We recommend the "youth hostel" in Plakiás *(yhplakias.com)* on the south coast.

BEACHES

Many beaches are only cleaned in front of hotels and where sun loungers and parasols are for hire. Lifeguards are only to be found on the most popular beaches and mainly during peak season only. Seaweed that has washed onto the beach at the beginning of the season is often only removed in May or June. Bathing shoes are recommended on many of the beaches (especially in summer when the sand tends to get extremely hot). Nude bathing is prohibited, but is practised on many isolated beaches. The only official nudist beach in Crete lies west of Chóra Sfakíon, at the only nudist hotel in Greece, *Hotel Vritomártis*. Topless sunbathing is accepted everywhere.

CLIMATE TAX & MUSEUM PRICE RISES

Since 2024, Greece has levied a climate tax on tourist overnight stays, graded according to category. From March to October, the tax is 1.50 euros for guesthouses, apartments and one- or two-star hotels; 3 euros for three-star hotels, 7 euros for four stars, and 10 euros for five-star establishments. From November to February the tax is 0.50–4 euros. As this guide went to press, a country-wide increase in the ticket price for state museums and archaeological sites was being considered. The rise is visitor-number dependent; so, for example, an entrance ticket for Knossós, Crete's most-visited archaeological site, and for Spinalónga would rise to 20 euros each; entrance to the Diktéon Ándron stalactite cave would rise to 15 euros. It is always worth double-checking entrance prices before you visit.

CUSTOMS

EU citizens can import and export goods for their personal use tax-free (but only 800 cigarettes, 90 litres of wine, 10 litres of spirits). Visitors from the UK must observe the following limits: 200 cigarettes or 50 cigars or 250g tobacco; 4 litres of spirits (over 22% vol.), or 9 litres of spirits (under 22% vol.), 18 litres of (still)wine. For more information go to *gov.uk*.

DRINKING WATER

You can drink the (chlorinated) tap water everywhere except Iráklio. Still mineral water *(metallikó neró)* is also available in restaurants and cafés and is usually the same price as in the supermarkets.

EARTHQUAKES

Light earthquakes do occur occasionally and are no reason to panic. Should you experience one, take cover underneath a door frame, a table or a bed. As soon as the quake is over you should go outside (but do not use the lifts) and then stay clear of walls and flower pots that might topple over. Once outside follow the lead of the locals.

Electricity

You will need a UK–EU adapter for your devices.

FIRES

Wildfires are a risk on Crete, especially on warm and windy days. Usually, they are extinguished quickly, and no one is harmed. If there's a higher risk than usual, then the population is warned in advance; in this situation, it's best to do whaever the locals do.

INTERNET & WIFI

Almost all hotels, bars, cafés and tavernas offer free wifi.

LANGUAGE

The Greeks are very proud of their language characters which are unique to Greece. More and more place names are being written in Roman letters as well, but it is still helpful to have some knowledge of the Greek alphabet (see p. 153). However, there is no uniform transliteration, so don't be surprised if you encounter four different versions of a place name .

Sometimes the correct accents on addresses, hotel and restaurant names are missing in this guide. The

GREEK ALPHABET

A	α	a		N	ν	n
B	β	v, w		Ξ	ξ	ks, x
Γ	γ	g, i		O	o	o
Δ	δ	d		Π	π	p
E	ε	e		P	ρ	r
Z	ζ	s, z		Σ	σ, ς	s, ss
H	η	i		T	τ	t
Θ	θ	th		Y	υ	i, y
I	ι	i, j		Φ	φ	f
K	κ	k		X	χ	ch
Λ	λ	l		Ψ	ψ	ps
M	μ	m		Ω	ώ	o

HOW MUCH DOES IT COST?

Boat tour	20 to 40 euros *all day, without transfer*
Coffee	1.50 to 3 euros *for an espresso/mocha*
Gyros	3.50 to 5 euros *for gyros and pitta*
Wine	3 to 7 euros *for a glass of wine*
Petrol	2.30 euros *for a litre of unleaded petrol*
Deckchairs	7 to 15 euros *per day for two people including parasol*

locals often don't know them anyway; they seldom call places by their official names and are used to calling hotels and tavernas according to the owner's name. When giving addresses, it is better to name landmarks rather than a street name. No accents are used locally when writing in Latin script, so don't input accents into your SatNav.

MONEY & CREDIT CARDS

The national currency is the euro and the cents are called *leptá*. Bank opening hours are Monday–Thursday 8am–2pm, Friday 8am–1.30pm. Cash machines are plentiful.

PHOTOGRAPHY

Taking photographs of military installations is strictly prohibited and the respective signs must absolutely be observed. Over the years, quite a number of foreigners have spent many weeks behind bars because they were spotted taking pictures of military jets during take-off or landing.

POST

There are post offices in all cities and larger villages, open Mon–Fri 7.30am–1.30pm. In the tourism centres they sometimes open until 8.30pm.

PUBLIC HOLIDAYS

1 Jan	New Year's Day
6 Jan	Epiphany
Feb/March	Réthimno Carnival
Feb/March	Shrove Monday
25 March	Independence Day
March/April	Good Friday
March/April	Easter
1 May	Labour Day
Late May	Whitsun
June	Mátala Beach Festival
15 Aug	Assumption Day
Oct	Réthimno Renaissance Carnival
28 Oct	National holiday
25/26 Dec	Christmas

SHOP OPENING HOURS

In the resorts most shops open daily from 10am to 11pm. In the towns and cities, shops with a predominantly local customer base are open Monday–Saturday at least 10am–2pm and Tuesday, Thursday, Friday also from 5.30–9pm.

TELEPHONE COUNTRY CODES

Greece *0030;* UK *0044;* United States *001;* Australia *0061.*

TIPPING

Tips for good service are appreciated in all restaurants. Greeks tend to give a lot occasionally rather than too little regularly; small tips under 50 cents are seen as an insult. Tips are left on the table when leaving.

TOILETS

Many of Crete's toilets can be very posh and equipped with the latest Italian sanitary installations. However, be aware that even here and in the good hotels you are not allowed to flush the used toilet paper down the drain, but have to throw it in the bin provided. The reason for this is that the paper clogs the often narrow drains and septic tanks.

TOURIST INFORMATION

Local tourist information offices (available in Ágios Nikólaos, Chaniá, Iráklio and Sitía) are often of little help and do not act as agents for accommodation or event tickets.

WEATHER IN IRÁKLIO

■ High season
■ Low season

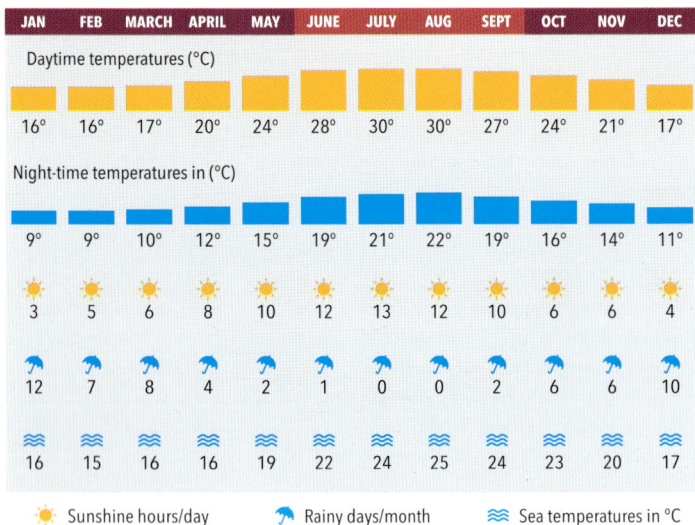

	JAN	FEB	MARCH	APRIL	MAY	JUNE	JULY	AUG	SEPT	OCT	NOV	DEC
Daytime temperatures (°C)	16°	16°	17°	20°	24°	28°	30°	30°	27°	24°	21°	17°
Night-time temperatures in (°C)	9°	9°	10°	12°	15°	19°	21°	22°	19°	16°	14°	11°
Sunshine hours/day	3	5	6	8	10	12	13	12	10	6	6	4
Rainy days/month	12	7	8	4	2	1	0	0	2	6	6	10
Sea temperatures in °C	16	15	16	16	19	22	24	25	24	23	20	17

☀ Sunshine hours/day   🌂 Rainy days/month   ≋ Sea temperatures in °C

USEFUL WORDS
& PHRASES

SMALLTALK

Yes/no/maybe	neˈochi/ˈissos	Ναι/ Όχι/Ισως
Please/Thank you	parakaˈlo/efcharisˈto	Παρακαλώ/ Ευχαριστώ
Good morning/good evening/goodnight!	kalliˈmera/kalliˈspera/ kalliˈnichta!	Καλημέραμ/ Καλησπέρα!/ Καληνύχτα!
Hello/ goodbye (formal)/ goodbye (informal)!	ˈya (su/sass)/ aˈdio/ ya (su/sass)!	Γεία (σου/σας)!/ αντίο!/Γεία (σου/ σας)!
My name is …	me ˈlene …	Με λένεÖ …
What's your name?	poss sass ˈlene?	Πως σας λένε?
Excuse me/sorry	me sigˈchorite/ sigˈnomi	Με συγχωρείτε / Συγνώημ
Pardon?	oˈriste?	Ορίστε?
I (don't) like this	Afˈto (dhen) mu aˈressi	Αυτό (δεν) ουμ αρέσει

EATING & DRINKING

Could you please book a table for tonight for four?	Klisˈte mass parakaˈlo ˈenna traˈpezi ya aˈpopse ya ˈtessera ˈatoma	Κλείστε αςμ παρακαλώ ένα τραπέζι γιά απόψε γιά τέσσερα άτοαμ
The menu, please	tonn kaˈtaloggo parakaˈlo	Τον κατάλογο παρακαλώ
Could I please have … ?	tha ˈithella na ˈecho …?	Θα ήθελα να έχο …?
more/less	pjo/liˈgotäre	ρπιό/λιγότερο
with/without ice/ sparkling	me/choˈris ˈpa-go/ anthrakikˈko	εμ/χωρίς πάγο/ ανθρακικό
(un)safe drinking water	(mi) ˈpossimo nä̃ro	(μη) Πόσιμο νερό
vegetarian/allergy	chortoˈfagos/allergˈia	Χορτοφάγος/ Αλλεργία
May I have the bill, please?	ˈthelˈlo na pliˈrosso parakaˈlo	Θέλω να πληρώσω παρακαλώ

HOLIDAY VIBES

FOR RELAXATION & CHILLING

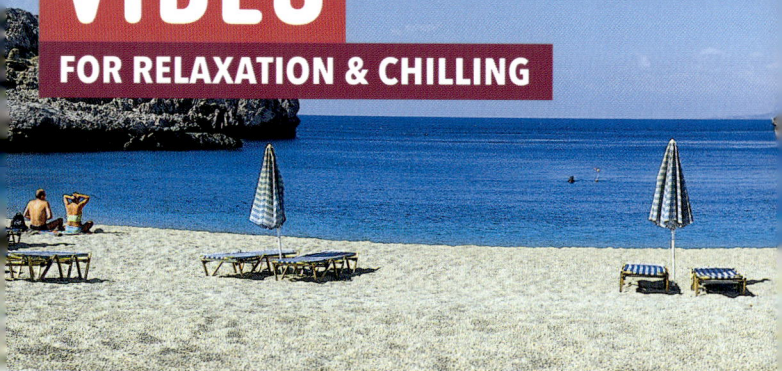

FOR BOOKWORMS & FILM BUFFS

ZORBA THE GREEK

A Cretan classic (both book and film), written by Níkos Kazantzákis and directed by Michael Cacoyannis in 1964. Starring Anthony Quinn and Irene Pappas, it created the archetypal Cretan and still radiates a strong feeling of Cretan *joie de vivre*.

THE ISLAND

This historical novel by award-winning author Victoria Hislop is set on the former leper colony of Spinalónga, an island off the Cretan coast.

HE WHO MUST DIE

A 1956 film directed by Jules Dassin based on the novel *Christ Recrucified* by Níkos Kazantzákis and filmed mainly in Krítsa. It starred Melina Mercouri and Gert Fröbe. The topic has become current again: the plight of migrants.

THE DARK LABYRINTH

Lawrence Durrell didn't only write about Corfu. This captivating novel is set on Crete just after World War II, when a variety of English cruise-ship passengers come ashore to explore, with dramatic consequences.

PLAYLIST

0:58

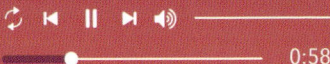

‖ XYLOURIS WHITE – DAPHNE
Cretan *lýra* player George Xylouris and Australian drummer Jim White combine Cretan music with rock and free jazz.

▶ PSARANTONIS & PSARONIKOS – O DIAS
Brothers Antónis and Níkos Xylouris are regarded as the grand masters of Cretan *lýra* music.

▶ ROSS DALY – EROTOKRITOS
This Irishman who lives on Crete is a traditional musician who has developed his very own version of the *lýra*.

▶ ADAEIS – NTROPI
This band, founded in Iráklio in 2015, plays rock music with Greek lyrics.

▶ NANA MOUSKOURI – THE WHITE ROSE OF ATHENS
The global star was born in Chaniá.

*Your holiday soundtrack can be found on **Spotify** under **MARCO POLO** Greece*

Or scan this code with the Spotify app

ONLINE

CRETE TV
Many films made in and featuring Crete are streamed live around the clock at cretetv.gr.

CRETAN BEACHES
This app describes more than 300 beaches on the island in great detail (in English).

HERSONISSOS LIFE
Are you wondering what to do tonight? This app gives recommendations on how to spend the evening in the best clubs on Crete (in English).

MY CRETE GUIDE
Best-rated travel app for Crete, with personalised information across 40 categories, including the E4 hiking trail. For Android, free.

LIVING IN CRETE
Website about expat life on Crete: livingincrete.net

GREEK MYTHOLOGY
Website (*greekmythology.com*) and app (for iOS and Android) all about the Greek myths, including specific information about the stories based on Crete.

INDEX

WE WANT TO HEAR FROM YOU!

Did you have a great holiday? Is there something on your mind? Whatever it is, let us know! Whether you want to praise the guide, alert us to errors or give us a personal tip – MARCO POLO would be pleased to hear from you.

We do everything we can to provide the very latest information for your trip. Nevertheless, despite all of our authors' thorough research, errors can creep in. MARCO POLO does not accept any liability for this. Please contact us by e-mail.

e-mail: sales@heartwoodpublishing.co.uk

Picture credits
Cover: Loutró (AWL: St. Outram)
Photos: DuMont Bildarchiv: T. Gerber (58/59); huber-images: G. Croppi (126), J. Huber (118/119), Mehlig (16/17), R. Schmid (74/75, 81, 94/95), A. Serrano (21), G. Simeone (68/69), M. Simoni (2/3, 72); huber-images/SIME: R. Spila (128/129); Laif: T. Gerber (37, 66, 71, 87, 88/89, 104/105, 138), C. Heeb (108/109), D. Schwelle (13); Laif/hemis.fr: B. Gardel (34/35); Laif/Lo Figaro Magazine: Fabre (53); Laif/robertharding: T. Auzins (8/9, 14/15, 26/27), S. Black (50/51, 148/149); mauritius images: R. Hackenberg (82, 116), M. Simoni (85), Tschanz-Hofmann (33); mauritius images/Alamy (29, 40/41), D. Crossland (122), O. Danileiko (28/29), G. B. Evans (64), B. Forenius (12), S. Kaczmarczyk (102), S. Lubenow (92), A. McAulay (front cover flap), H. Milas (54, 115), S. Outram (30), B. Petkovic (132/133), G. Tsichlis (62, 112); mauritius images/Alamy/a-plus bank (32/33); mauritius images/Alamy/Delphotos (56); mauritius images/Alamy/Hackenberg-Photo-Cologne (44, 130); mauritius images/Alamy/Jayskyland Images (48); mauritius images/Hemis.fr: F. Guiziou (11, 143, 144), R. Mattes (6/7); mauritius images/imagebroker: M. Breuer (98); mauritius images/imageBROKER: R. Franken (22), F. Schneider (137); mauritius images/John Warburton-Lee: K. Kreder (back cover flap); mauritius images/Nature in Stock: E. Ruiterman (25); picture alliance/DUMONT Bildarchiv (106); shutterstock: C. Badkin (10), A. Nekrassov (91); O. Stadler (156/157); K. Verigou (159)

5th Edition – fully revised and updated 2025
Worldwide Distribution: Heartwood Publishing Ltd, Bath, United Kingdom
www.heartwoodpublishing.co.uk

© MAIRDUMONT GmbH & Co. KG, Ostfildern
Authors: Klaus Bötig, Klio Verigou; **Editor**: Christina Sothmann
Picture editor: Barbara Mehrl
Cartography: © KOMPASS-Karten GmbH, A-6020 Innsbruck/MAIRDUMONT, D 73760 Ostfildern (pp 38-39, 134-135, 139, 141, 145, 147, pull-out map); © KOMPASS-Karten GmbH, kompass.de under licence from © OpenStreetMap Contributors, osm.org/copyright (pp. 42-43, 47, 60-61, 65, 76-77, 79, 94-95, 99, 110-111, 120-121, 124).
Cover design and pull-out map cover design: Eggers+Diaper, Aachen
Page designs: Langenstein Communication GmbH, Ludwigsburg

Heartwood Publishing credits:
Translated from the German by: Sophie Blacksell Jones, Thomas Moser, Wendy Barrow, Susan Jones, Jennifer Walcoff Neuheiser and Mo Croasdale
Editors: Felicity Laughton, Kate Michell
Prepress: Summerlane Books, Bath
Printed in India

MARCO POLO AUTHOR
KLIO VERIGOU

Even as a child, Klio enjoyed telling stories about her holidays on Crete, the birthplace of her father. After studying at RWTH Aachen University, she had the idea of bringing together her love for both Greece and Germany. As a travel journalist with Greek roots, she enjoys making new discoveries about Crete, but she also joins in with the family olive harvest and meets friends for cocktails in the island's beach bars.

DOS & DON'TS

HOW TO AVOID SLIP-UPS & BLUNDERS

DO BE CAREFUL WHEN ORDERING FISH

Fresh fish and shellfish are expensive and often sold by weight. Always ask for the kilo price first and when the fish is being weighed, make sure you are present to avoid any unpleasant surprises on the bill.

DON'T DRIVE OFF-ROAD

If you are travelling with a hired vehicle and leave the main road, you will be driving without insurance and will have to pay for any damages yourself. That sometimes even goes for 4×4 vehicles! Tyre damage is not insured most of the time, even if the damage occurred on a tarmac road.

DON'T RISK A FOREST FIRE

The risk of a forest fire on Crete is high. Smokers must be especially careful when disposing of their cigarette butts. Broken glass can also ignite a fire.

DON'T COLLECT YOUR OWN SOUVENIRS

On the beach and in the mountains, no one will mind if you collect a pebble or two, but taking a stone that has been crafted into something or ceramic shards from an archaeological site is a criminal offence.